NONONSEN

SACRAMENTO PUBLIC LIBRARY
828 "I" Street

D0402286

HOW TO
FIND WORK
YOU LOVE

About the author

Paul Allen is a journalist and editor from London who now lives in Brighton. He writes about the voluntary sector for *The Guardian*, has run environmental projects for the BBC, and helped charities like Macmillan Cancer Support find their tone of voice. In 2007, he wrote *Your Ethical Business*, a start-up guide to creating a socially and environmentally responsible business. Today, he runs his own company, Lark (larkagency.com), which helps organizations put their stories into the right words.

Acknowledgements

A huge thank you to all of the inspiring people who kindly shared their career experiences with me during the writing of this book.

Thanks to Anna Moore for her expert editorial judgment and support, to fellow Larks Sophie Ball and Chris Harding, and to Chris Harrison, Scott Welti and Jane Miller at Harrison Agency for the cover design. I'm also very grateful to Chris Brazier, Juha Sorsa, Jo Lateu and Dan Raymond-Barker at New Internationalist for their guidance, understanding and expertise, and to Kate Shepherd at Oxford Publicity Partnership.

Finally, thanks to Michael and Tricia Allen, who always encouraged me to find work I love.

NONONSENSE LIFE

THE ETHICAL CAREERS GUIDE

HOW TO FIND WORK YOU LOVE

PAUL ALLEN

New Internationalist

NONONSENSE LIFE
The Ethical Careers Guide
How To Find Work You Love

Published in 2017 by
New Internationalist Publications Ltd
The Old Music Hall
106-108 Cowley Road
Oxford OX4, 1JE, UK
newint.org

© Paul Allen
The right of Paul Allen to be identified as the author of this work has been asserted in
accordance with the Copyright, Designs and Patents Act 1998.

All rights reserved. No part of this book may be reproduced, stored in a retrieval system
or transmitted, in any form or by any means, electronic, electrostatic, magnetic tape,
mechanical, photocopying, recording or otherwise, without prior permission in writing
from the Publisher.

Series editor: Chris Brazier
Cover concept: Harrison Agency
Internal design: Juha Sorsa

Printed and bound in the Czech Republic by PBtisk, who hold environmental
accreditation ISO 14001.

British Library Cataloguing-in-Publication-Data.
A catalogue record for this book is available from the British Library.

ISBN 978-1-78026-322-9
(ISBN ebook 978-1-78026-323-6)

Picture credits: author photo, James Lambie; p10, Allis Sinisalu; p18, FatCamera/
Thinkstock; p32, hxdbzxy/Thinkstock; p52, Austin Ban; p66, Creative Commons;
p86, g-stockstudio/Thinkstock; p88, Patrik Göthe; p101, marekuliasz/Thinkstock;
p106, Andrea Boldizsar; p119, Creative Commons; p134, Creative Commons;
p148 kgtoh/Thinkstock.

For Magnus and Zach

Contents

Introduction

Introduction

You will spend around 100,000 hours of your life at work.

It's a long time to be doing something you don't like.

We have many expectations about our working lives – but making a positive difference is often ignored. Most job adverts will tell you about salary, hours and career progression, but they usually don't say much about the change you could make to other people's lives or the planet.

If you care about using your time at work to make a positive impact on the world, this is the book for you. The good news is you're not alone – in fact it seems that an increasing number of us are putting principles above profit.

The 2016 Deloitte Millennial Survey is one of many recent studies which show our growing desire for more ethical working lives.[1]

Almost half of the 7,700 young people surveyed across 29 countries said they had turned down a job offer because the company's values did not match their own. A similar amount said they had rejected assignments at work because of conflicts with their ethics – and over half had sworn never to work for specific companies because of the organizations' values.

In total, 87 per cent of people said a company's success should not be measured purely by its financial performance, and should include 'a larger purpose'.

More than money

Ethical jobs don't just benefit others – they also help us.

Some of us see fulfilment, or even happiness, as a by-product of earning a good wage. If we can only earn enough, we can 'buy' ourselves satisfaction.

---

1 Deloitte Millennial Survey, nin.tl/deloitteyouth

That simply isn't true. Many academic studies have shown that, over a certain baseline, earning more money doesn't make you any happier. Yes, you'll have more 'stuff', live in a bigger house, or drive a more expensive car. But it won't make you any happier with life.

So what will? The answer lies in making the most of our working lives.

> The longer our products last, the less impact they will have on the environment, and the bigger our smile will be.

When British entrepreneurs David and Claire Heiatt started their clothing business Howies in 1995, they talked about the 'rocking-chair test', their personal measure of being a good company:

'Every product we make has passed the rocking-chair test. When we are old and grey and sitting in our rocking chairs, we can look back on the company we created with a smile.

'That's why we go to the trouble of using the best-quality materials to make sure our clothing lasts longer. The longer our products last, the less impact they will have on the environment, and the bigger our smile will be.'

Work you love

There isn't a single formula for finding a brilliant ethical career. Instead, there are lots of them, and they all hinge on one unique factor. You.

But even if we are all different, there's always a common factor in any ethical job.

Whether you want to spend your time working in marine conservation or in website design, an ethical job is always rooted in a purpose. And there are always two possible beneficiaries: people or planet.

People

The first is about people – does your job help others?

A classic example would be a nurse or doctor, or working for an anti-poverty charity. But there are many other ways to make a difference. For example, you could work for a digital innovation business that aims to use new technology to improve disadvantaged people's access to healthcare.

You can define 'people' as narrowly or broadly as you like. Some of us feel best making a difference to the lives of a relatively small number of people, say in our local community. For others, this could be about a much larger number – even everyone on the planet.

Planet

The second element is planet, or environmental impact.

As with people, this could mean helping to make small-scale changes – such as a local conservation issue – or a far bigger, global goal. It embraces everything from protecting habitats and wildlife to improving biodiversity and developing clean-fuel technology.

Often there's no clear distinction between people and planet – and it really is just a single 'purpose'.

For example, the challenges around tackling climate change have increasingly led to very varied organizations – from humanitarian aid agencies to environmental campaigners – working together.

The third P

There's another 'p' we shouldn't overlook: profit.

This book is about helping you find a career. It's not about giving your time away for nothing (even if volunteering can be a great stepping stone – more on that later).

Sometimes there is a financial sacrifice in choosing an ethical career. But it's also possible to earn the same (or more) by sticking to your principles. We'll look at a range of ethically motivated jobs throughout the book from the people who have been there and done it.

Reality check

For many of us, working can feel like a means to an end – a pay cheque at the end of the week or month.

Any paid job can be hard to find – and we often can't afford to be picky. And even when you are working, how can you change the way a business runs? You might want to make a difference and add an ethical dimension to your company, but what if you don't have any power?

According to the Office for National Statistics, over 800,000 people in the UK are currently working on zero-hour contracts – which means they have little security, say or benefits at work.[2] In difficult economic times, there is a danger that 'ethical careers' can feel too idealistic, or that they are only for people with enough money not to worry about making ends meet: a lifestyle choice for the comfortably well off.

This is not true.

Yes, some people may find it easier to move from unsatisfying work to a more meaningful career. And sometimes money can help. For example, being able to take some time out, scale back on the 9-to-5 grind, or take up a new course of study.

Whatever your situation, this book doesn't assume you can simply give it all up, or fall into your perfect job tomorrow. Rather, it aims to act as a stepping stone – to give you the practical ideas, confidence and understanding to make a difference to your working life.

You'll find advice on how to get started and where to focus your energy. And along the way you'll meet many different people, from all walks of life, who have – in one way or another – gone against the grain, and made their jobs 'work' just that bit better for them.

---

2 Office for National Statistics, nin.tl/zerohourscontracts

Whether you're looking to make small changes or to take a leap into the unknown, the material here should help you to look ahead with confidence. It can sometimes take a little while to get to where you want to be – but the fact that you're reading this book is a great first step.

How to use this book

There is no right way to read this book. For some instant inspiration, you can dip in and out of sections, read about some interesting people who have found work they love, and find practical resources that can help you on your journey.

The only 'rule' is to read the next chapter. It's called 'Getting to know you' – and it'll help you to decide what you really want out of an ethical career. Unless you already have a very clear plan, it's a good way to set some boundaries and not feel overwhelmed by the options.

One final note. You may not always get it right and that's fine too. This is a 'careers' guide, and that's deliberately plural. It's very rare to find your dream job first time around. But every new working experience will help you learn more about what matters to you – and how you should be spending those 100,000 precious hours.

'You have one job.
And that is to live an
extraordinary life.'

Umair Haque

2

Getting to know you

Identifying what matters most

Getting to know you

There are more than one billion Google hits for the word 'career', but none of them can promise you one that makes a positive difference.

Defining that 'difference' is very personal. We are all unique; we all have different ideas of what really matters – and what's worth working for. And that means we need to start this book with some soul-searching.

Your priorities

This chapter is about discovering what matters most to you. It's not about drafting a five-year plan or pretending to know all the answers. And although we're starting with some introspection, this book isn't about spiritual discovery.

It's not a life-coaching course, or an exercise in finding your inner warrior, tiger, or anything else. It's a clear, pragmatic and practical guide that will hopefully help you find the answers to some fundamental career questions.

The more you know what matters to you, the better you'll be able to judge the opportunities out there – and create new ones for yourself in the workplace.

The right path

This chapter cannot cover absolutely everything. There may be additional personal questions for you to consider, which will help you on the right path. The important thing is for you to identify what really matters to you in the workplace, and what's less significant. It's about setting your priorities and defining the 'purpose' in an ethical career.

Let's get started

How do you find a job that ticks all of your boxes? The first step is to work out what those boxes are, and how much each one really matters.

After all, one person's idea of an amazing ethical career might be your idea of falling short, or selling out. There is no one size fits all.

For this exercise, grab a pencil and paper, and get ready to write.

Step 1: Your passions

First, look at the list on the following two pages. These are the possible causes that you could support through your working life.

Remember that you could do this in many different ways.

For example, if you're passionate about clean energy, you could get a job at an environmental charity – but you could also work for a profit-making firm that sponsors green tech innovation. For now, don't worry too much about 'how' you'll help, just think about the areas that most interest you. There are some blank rows at the bottom so you can add any extras that have not been included here.

For some people, this is a very simple exercise – especially if they have a strong personal connection to a particular issue. If this sounds like you, it's good news. We know that feeling passionately about a particular cause or concern is a huge motivator – it can help you find a job in the first place, and ensure you love the work you do.

For most of us, there are more grey areas – and that's okay too. We don't all have clear passions, and may be open to a range of causes. That's normal. For example, many people in the charity sector move between very different causes during their careers (for example, from a breast-cancer charity to an animal-rescue organization). For them, the most important thing is the kind of role they're working in, and the fact they are making a positive difference to people's lives.

> For now, don't worry too much about 'how' you'll help, just think about the areas that most interest you.

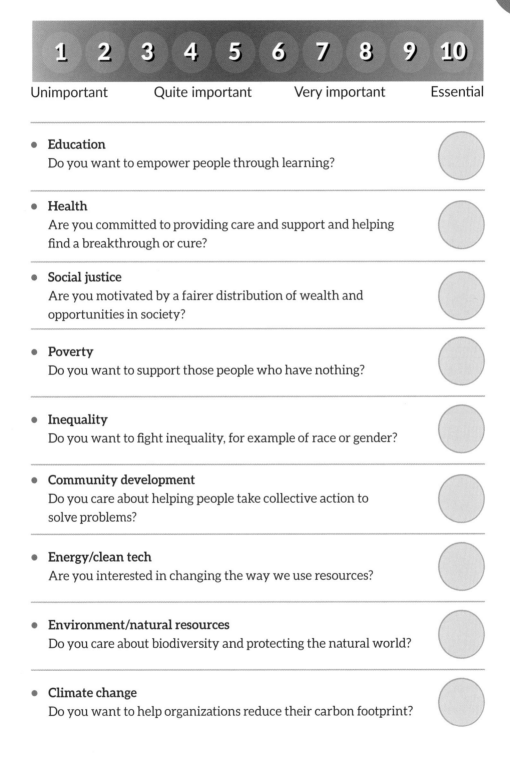

| 1 | 2 | 3 | 4 | 5 | 6 | 7 | 8 | 9 | 10 |

Unimportant   Quite important   Very important   Essential

- **Education**
  Do you want to empower people through learning?

- **Health**
  Are you committed to providing care and support and helping find a breakthrough or cure?

- **Social justice**
  Are you motivated by a fairer distribution of wealth and opportunities in society?

- **Poverty**
  Do you want to support those people who have nothing?

- **Inequality**
  Do you want to fight inequality, for example of race or gender?

- **Community development**
  Do you care about helping people take collective action to solve problems?

- **Energy/clean tech**
  Are you interested in changing the way we use resources?

- **Environment/natural resources**
  Do you care about biodiversity and protecting the natural world?

- **Climate change**
  Do you want to help organizations reduce their carbon footprint?

- **Sustainable agriculture**
  Are you interested in ensuring our food and other products are farmed in a way that is kind to the planet?

- **Animal welfare**
  Do you care about improving the treatment of animals?

- **Economic change**
  Do you want to help transform economies to become more sustainable in the long term?

- **International development**
  Do you want to help improve lives in the developing world?

- **Fair trade**
  Do you want to help farmers and growers get a better deal in the market?

- **Corporate impact**
  Are you looking to transform the corporate world?

- **Faith**
  Is religion or faith important in deciding your focus?

- Add your own

- Add your own

Step 2: The 10 motivators

There's more to an ethical career than supporting the right cause. The next exercise is to rank 10 important characteristics of any ethical job. These will help you gain a better idea of how to decide which roles will suit you best.

| 1 | 2 | 3 | 4 | 5 | 6 | 7 | 8 | 9 | 10 |

Unimportant   Quite important   Very important   Essential

Motivator 1: Money

It may not be your *only* motivator, but it's likely to be a necessity. How much do financial rewards drive you? Does the idea of getting more money for better results – such as a performance-based bonus – give you a buzz? Would you sacrifice salary if it meant you could spent more time doing what you really love? Does earning a high wage help you to feel important? Is it something that gives you purpose, or are you just as comfortable in yourself if you earn less, as long as you're doing something meaningful?

Motivator 2: Impact

If you want your working life to make a difference to others, how important is the scale of that impact? Would you be happiest affecting a local issue where you can see the difference you're making – even if it's a small number of people or limited area? Or would you prefer to be further from the difference you're making on the ground if you could have a much greater impact? How important is it for your impact to be on a large scale?

Motivator 3: Individuality

How independent are you? Do you want to lead the charge, or are you more comfortable being part of a like-minded team? Some people thrive with support and guidance – such as having a mentor, being given a clear structure for their work and knowing their deadlines. Others find that approach to work too stifling – they don't like being told how to spend their time, prefer to go their own way, and are very self-motivated. How much of a lone operator are you?

Motivator 4: Proximity

Do you mind working behind the scenes, knowing that your efforts will make a difference – even if you're not the one delivering it on the ground? There are many career paths that help others, but are removed from the action. How much do you want to be out there working on the frontline, even if that could mean being in more pressurized or difficult work situations?

Motivator 5: Immediacy

How quickly do you need to see the fruits of your labour? Some ethical career paths give you lots of 'quick wins', while others are harder to see – and are much more about the long game.

For example, working at an animal-rescue charity could give you plenty of immediate rewards. Equally, if your company helps fund new hospitals or schools in conflict zones, you'll also be able to see the difference. By contrast, working for a climate-change NGO could be an immensely rewarding career – but there are often fewer tangible 'wins' to celebrate. How important is it for you to see quick results?

Motivator 6: Status and recognition

How much does status matter to you? This isn't just about money or material status symbols. For example, some people really value having a job title that reflects their influence and impact. Others may prefer to work only with (and for) high-profile organizations, industry leaders or household names. Is that you – or would you be happy to work for smaller organizations and businesses out of the limelight? Do you also need to be recognized for your achievements and skills – say by colleagues and other professionals? Or perhaps you're comfortable making a difference even without the accolades. Does recognition matter to you?

Motivator 7: Shared values

How important is the 'cause' to your idea of an ethical career? Could you work for an organization that isn't intrinsically set up to make a positive difference, but is still doing something good in the world?

Your decision here could affect the potential impact you make. For example, you may be more likely to make a bigger difference working in sustainability for a transnational corporation than for a very small charity. Some people would say this 'bigger picture' is more important than whether you share absolutely all of the company's values. Other people would never want to make that compromise.

Are you happy to help change a corporate culture – or do you only want to work with like-minded people and organizations? How important are shared values?

Motivator 8: Expertise

People are often happiest when they're good at what they do. How much are you driven by a particular skill, qualification or specialism? For example, you may want to follow an established profession – such as medicine, engineering, law or accountancy.

Do you like the idea of being a specialist – knowing a lot about one particular area – and people calling on you for that expert opinion? Or do you prefer the idea of being more generalist – picking up a wider range of skills and experiences, but perhaps less expertise? How important is it for you to follow a particular specialism?

Motivator 9: Balance

How much do you want to keep your career separate from your personal life? When work becomes a passion, these can blur – which is fine for some people but not for others. If your job is based around a particular cause, there can also be additional pressure to put this above your private life. Are you the kind of person who is happy to put heart and soul into your job, or do you want a clearer line between work and home – and an employer who will recognize and respect that? As well as emotional pressure, this is also about the practical stuff, such as being able to work part-time, flexible hours, the ability to work from home, and having a short or easy commute. How important is balance?

Motivator 10: Business

Do you think you would like to start your own company one day? This could be something you realize (and decide) later on, but if you're already planning on starting a business, this may affect your career paths and the experiences you seek out – for example, you could cherry pick the right place to learn what you need to strike out on your own. Equally, if you know that you don't want the responsibility of running an organization, this can also help you narrow down the right options. Could you see yourself running your own business?

Your score

Now check back over your answers and look for the extremes – where you've given either a very high or low mark to a motivator.

This can help you build a picture of the kind of work that will give you the greatest satisfaction. Whenever you research and apply for positions, make sure you find out as much as you can about the role and organization, and use these criteria to judge how well they fit your values and priorities.

What's good enough?

How many of your passion and motivator 'boxes' should a job tick? Author and career coach John Lees suggests that you should be happy with a 70-per-cent match.

In other words, compare all of the career passions and motivators that you've noted in this chapter about what matters to you, and compare it with the 'shopping list' of what your potential employer is looking for.

You'll likely need to look beyond the job description. If you can, it's a great idea to talk to someone close to the organization to get a better sense of the role, and what it's really like to work there.

Clearly, you want the employer and job to match up with your criteria, but 'don't get carried away with the idea of a perfect job,' writes Lees.

'If you identify a genuine overlap of around 70 per cent, the job will probably be a good match...

'If it feels more like 50-60 per cent, it may be an acceptable stepping-stone. [But] if the match is 50 per cent or less, watch out.'

Theory to reality

Now you know much more about what matters to you, how do you find a job that matches? In practice, landing your dream role depends on three factors, as you can see in the following diagram.

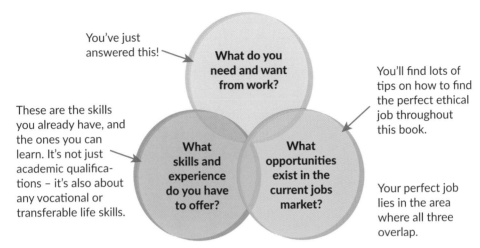

You've just answered this!

What do you need and want from work?

These are the skills you already have, and the ones you can learn. It's not just academic qualifications – it's also about any vocational or transferable life skills.

What skills and experience do you have to offer?

What opportunities exist in the current jobs market?

You'll find lots of tips on how to find the perfect ethical job throughout this book.

Your perfect job lies in the area where all three overlap.

Trust your instincts?

Perhaps surprisingly, there's strong evidence to show that we're not actually very good at predicting what will make us happy.

For example, most people say that more money is the one thing that will improve the quality of their life. But all the evidence shows a pretty weak connection between income and both life and job satisfaction. (See *Stumbling on Happiness* by psychologist Daniel Gilbert, among others.)

This doesn't mean you should discount everything you've thought about. But it's good to recognize that we're all likely to bring some personal bias. In particular, we're likely to think that we're 'different' – and won't have the same experiences as others. In some ways, this is a good trait; it helps us make decisions and feel optimistic.

But it can also lead us to disappointment, especially if we follow career paths without our eyes wide open.

Real-life experience

The best way to check your assumptions will always be to give something a go. There's no substitute for actually doing the job.

The reality may be different from your expectations – sometimes for better, sometimes for worse. But even if things don't go to plan, you'll always learn something. Often jobs will open up new opportunities and you may be surprised to discover certain things you're particularly good at, or especially like (or dislike!). It's all useful experience.

Ethical shortcut

Here's a useful shortcut for your passions and motivators. The non-profit 'effective altruism' research organization 80,000 Hours believes the four most important factors for predicting job satisfaction are:

1 **Engaging, meaningful work:** the extent to which you have variety, autonomy, a sense of completion, feedback and work that you feel makes a difference.

2 **Getting on with your colleagues:** the extent to which you get help from, like and form meaningful relationships with your colleagues.

3 **Personal fit:** the extent to which you're likely to be good at your job, are interested in the content, and are able to use your signature strengths.

4 **Hygiene factors:** do you have reasonable hours, job security, a short commute and sufficient pay?[1]

  1 80,000 Hours, nin.tl/jobsuit

Doer or Changer?

In this chapter, we've spent a lot of time thinking about your personal motivations. Throughout the rest of the book, we'll look at how this understanding can help you navigate a world of career choices.

To make that job easier, we have divided ethical careers into two different approaches:

Doers Some jobs seem intrinsically ethical. You may have your heart set, for example, on working for an environmental charity, or a humanitarian NGO. Or you may pursue a career that exists to help others, such as a nurse or a vet. By choosing this path, or aligning yourself to a cause or organization that has positive change at its very core, your choice of career will always be rooted in ethical values. If this sounds like you, the next chapter will be particularly valuable. It's called 'The Doers'.

Changers Other jobs are less obviously ethical. From an accountant to a web developer, you could put almost every 'regular' job into this pot. Although they aren't intrinsically 'ethical', across the UK (and the globe) a growing number of people have transformed these ordinary career paths – showing many amazing ways that you can turn a for-profit company into a force for good. If that approach interests you, the subsequent chapter should give you lots of inspiration. It's called 'The Changers'.

One final note: If you're motivated by any career challenge that makes a meaningful difference to people's lives or the planet, it may be that you can move very easily between these two approaches – and that this distinction isn't so relevant. And that's fine too.

The most important thing is to show you the many different options available for pursuing an ethical career, and inspire you to take the next step.

"I think you are out of your mind if you keep taking jobs that you don't like because you think it will look good on your resumé. Isn't that a little like saving up sex for your old age?"

Warren Buffett

3 The Doers

Exploring the world of charities, NGOs and social enterprises

The Doers

Do you want to work for an organization whose *only* purpose is to make a positive difference in the world – whether that's helping other people or protecting our planet?

There are thousands of brilliant organizations around the world which are rooted in ethical principles – and aren't just about making people rich. No matter what experience you have, or what you're good at, you could join them.

Take the Red Cross, one of the world's most famous charities. For more than 150 years, it has supported millions of people in crisis across the globe.

Today, over 3,000 people work for the British branch of the Red Cross alone.

They're not all on the front line, handing out urgent supplies or giving medical care. Behind the scenes, the Red Cross needs thousands of people with an incredibly wide-ranging set of skills and experiences – from IT experts and accountants to designers, marketing professionals and lawyers. But even if the back-office teams aren't flying out to the crisis zones, they are still contributing towards the wider goal.

A good cause

I would call everyone working at the Red Cross a 'doer'. Just by doing their job – and collectively helping the charity to achieve its mission – they are making a positive impact on the world. Paid as professionals and working for an organization that alleviates suffering, it's the definition of an ethical career.

If your moral compass points clearly towards working only for organizations which are aligned with your ethical values, a charity could be the perfect career choice.

There are thousands of charitable organizations, just like the Red Cross, which are rooted in a particular purpose or mission.

From animal protection and disability rights to architectural heritage and healthcare, there is an incredible range of causes that you can support through your working life.

We cannot capture every one here, but this chapter will guide you through the main kinds of 'doer' organization.

We hope you'll come out the other side feeling more informed and inspired – and better prepared to take your next step.

Getting your bearings

One of the hardest things when looking for an ethical job is simply knowing what's out there.

Whenever charity professionals are interviewed about their work, a surprisingly common line is: 'I didn't know there was a job like this.' But perhaps it shouldn't be such a surprise. After all, there are thousands of different kinds of ethically minded organizations in the UK, and a myriad of roles within each one.

If you want to make the right choices, you first need to understand the possible career paths available.

If you're just starting out from school or university, this should also help you to get a sense of the bigger career picture. After all, your ideal role may require a few jumps – perhaps you'll need to take a few stepping-stone jobs first to develop the skills and experience you need to get to where you really want to be.

If you're switching careers, you may be surprised at the different ways you can draw on your existing skills and experience – to find new challenges and opportunities at work.

In this section, we'll look at the two main career paths for any 'doer':

- Charities
- Social enterprises

'I'd rather spend my time doing something at least a bit useful'

Emma Livingston-Jones

Learning and Development Co-ordinator at the British Red Cross

Did you always want to work for a charity?

No, I didn't. There are so many differences between charities that I didn't really think of it as a sector. I really just wanted to do a job that was interesting. My first step was teaching with VSO [Voluntary Services Overseas] in Ethiopia. I agreed with their values, but it wasn't because it was a charity *per se*. If a private-sector organization had offered that role, I'd have done it too.

What was your motivation?

I was always interested in education and thought it could be a useful way to travel to different countries. I didn't feel I learned that much at university – I wanted to experience different people and cultures, and challenge myself.

What happened next?

I was teaching English as a foreign language in Ethiopia, which was good but didn't pay well. I found that regeneration was a good fit – as I could combine my training and education skills with the knowledge I'd picked up in Ethiopia about infrastructure. I found a job with another charity, BURA [the British Urban Regeneration Association], as learning and skills manager.

When that charity went bust...

Well, I had to find another job! For jobseekers, it's good to think about how resilient your charity will be to economic downturns. When the last property crash happened, all the money went from a lot of organizations. I started working at a very different charity, RIBA [Royal Institute of British Architects], and stayed there for four years.

What do you do now?

I work at the British Red Cross and project-manage training for delegates who work on emergency-response operations, such as the Nepal earthquake.

It is a passion or a job?

It is a job. But then we spend most of our lives doing our jobs, and I'd rather spend my time doing something that is interesting, first and foremost – and also at least a bit useful.

What's the NGO world really like?

I was a bit cynical about NGOs as I'd seen some negative consequences in Ethiopia. The reality is that it's very diverse. There are some highly professionalized organizations that do brilliant work, like the Red Cross, and some useless do-gooder organizations who actually do bad things. And even with the best intentions you can have bad projects. That said, I think the great things should be celebrated – and I see my role as helping to make things better and more efficient.

What advice would you give to someone starting out?

Be realistic and do your research. If you go in thinking it's all going to be perfect, I don't think the NGO sector is right for you. You definitely need to approach it with open eyes.

Personally, I also wish I'd had more of a plan. If I'd been more focused, moved a bit quicker between jobs, and thought more about the skills I needed to develop to progress, I think I'd be slightly further ahead in my career now. If you're the kind of person who's good at making game-plans, that can really help.

Working for a charity

Charities are the most common kind of 'doer' organizations. And they're top of a lot of people's 'dream job' list.

There are currently over 160,000 registered charities in the UK – employing around 825,000 paid staff.

The third sector

If you're thinking of applying for a charity job – but don't know too much about the charity world, it's helpful to understand how they work.

The third sector (as it's often called) is incredibly diverse. It's not just about different sizes – from tiny local community groups to multi-million-pound organizations like Save the Children. It's also about how they work, and what they do.

Many of the UK's best-loved charities are there to help people or animals in need, or to protect the natural environment. The British Heart Foundation and Greenpeace are great examples.

But what about the Landmark Trust – an enterprising organization which restores historic buildings and rents them out as holiday homes?

Or Policy Change, a 'think tank' that aims to help create 'a stronger society and a more dynamic economy'? These are both registered charities too.

Charities span an incredible range of causes – and we hear very little about most of them.

Hidden giants

One of the UK's biggest charities (above household names such as Oxfam and Save the Children) is the Lloyds Register Foundation.

Few people may have heard of it, but in 2015 the Lloyds Register Foundation became the UK's first charity with an income over £1 billion. The charity itself focuses on funding science, education and engineering research.

The Wellcome Trust is another vast charity in terms of revenue. It is dedicated to improving health through science and research, and employs over 500 members of staff.

These are clearly not the kind of charities which will have volunteers shaking a collection tin outside your local shopping centre or will run a shop on the high street. But they are all registered charities – and, together, they employ thousands of people to help them achieve their missions.

David Lale knows more than most people about job opportunities in the charity sector. As chief executive of Charity People, a specialist charity recruitment agency, he has helped people find jobs in charities for over 25 years.

'The big charity brands have always been good at getting people's attention,' he says. 'And when you talk to jobseekers, they normally name five or six of those big charities that they'd like to work for – and that's it. There are almost 160,000 charities that have completely passed them by.'

At a glance: the UK voluntary sector

Size

£12.12 billion

The gross value added (GVA) of the UK voluntary sector – £12.2 billion – is comparable to the nominal **gross domestic product of Iceland**.

The UK voluntary sector employs approximately **827,000 people** – more than two and a half times the number Tesco employs, and over half the number working for the NHS.

Employment status

Part-time
312,969
(38%)

Full-time
513,619
(62%)

Gender

Male
279,258
(34%)

Female
547,253
(66%)

UK voluntary sector paid workforce (head count)

Location

There are more charities and higher concentrations of charities per head in **major urban areas** than in other less densely populated areas.

Charities registered in just **seven London boroughs** account for 6% of all charities but over 30% of all income for the sector

Beneficiaries of voluntary organizations by number of organizations and spending, 2013/14 (% of overall)

Scotland has more charities per thousand of the population than other parts of the UK.

In **England**, the Southwest has the highest number of charities per thousand of the population (3.2 per thousand) and the Northeast the lowest (1.7 per thousand).

London contains the highest percentage of larger voluntary organizations, with 28% of its charities having an annual income of more than £1 million.

Beneficiaries

Voluntary organizations exist to serve many different types of people as well as the environment, across the UK and internationally. Here are the most common beneficiaries of UK charities:

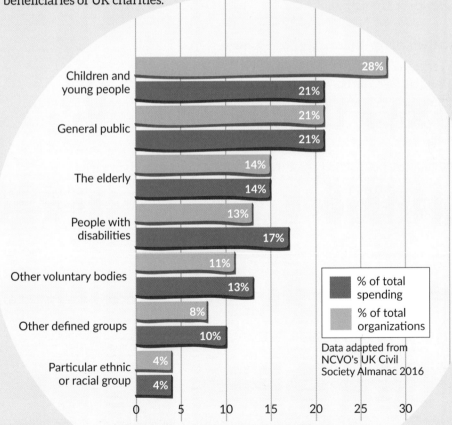

Beneficiaries of voluntary organizations by number of organizations and spending, 2013/14 (% of overall)

The 13 purposes

One of the reasons that charities are so incredibly diverse is that a 'charity' isn't technically a legal structure. From a local scout group to a global humanitarian organization, there are many ways to run a charity – some feel very small, local and informal, while others operate much more like a transnational business.

What every UK charity has in common is the need to exist 'for the public benefit' and meet at least one of 13 charitable purposes:

Education

Religion

Health or **saving lives**

Citizenship or **community development**

Arts, **culture**, **heritage** or **science**

Amateur sport

Human rights, **conflict resolution**, or promoting **religious or racial harmony or equality & diversity**

Environmental protection or **improvement**

Animal welfare

The armed forces, police, fire and rescue, or **ambulance services**

To relieve **people in need** due to youth, age, ill-health, disability, financial hardship or other disadvantage

To prevent **poverty**

Other – other charitable purposes: not explicitly mentioned above, but similar, such as rehabilitating ex-offenders and promoting mental welfare.

Foundations and trusts

For most of the UK's charities, raising enough money is a never-ending struggle. But one very powerful group of charities has a rather different financial challenge: how to spend it.

Some of the strongest organizations in the charity world – and the biggest employers – don't actually do the good work themselves. Instead, they enable others to do it.

There are around 8,800 charitable foundations in the UK, providing around £1.7 billion in grants to charitable causes each year.

The majority are known as 'grant-making trusts' – and their role is to manage money or property for charities. Often they are funded through an endowment – a large sum of money given to them by a family, individual or company. They often focus on just a few specific charitable areas, and divide the money up into a number of grants, for which charities can apply.

A tale of two trusts

The Volant Charitable Trust was set up in 2000 by author JK Rowling. Based in Edinburgh, its aim is to help charities combat poverty and social inequality, with a particular emphasis on women and children. Volant also funds major disaster appeals abroad. It can make grants of any size – typically over three years.

Three more inspirational women are behind **The Robertson Trust**, the largest independent grant-making trust in Scotland.

Instead of words and wizards, the Robertson sisters – Elspeth, Agnes and Ethel – made their fortune through whisky. The Glasgow-based family business is one of Scotland's largest private companies in the Scotch whisky industry, and owns The Famous Grouse and other whisky brands.

The sisters established their trust in 1961. To date, it has given more than £150 million to charities.

'I created and developed a role for myself and made sure they had to keep me on!'

Donna-Marie Steel

Training and Support Officer,
The Robertson Trust

Tell us a bit about what you do

I help deliver The Robertson Trust's special bursary programme. We give financial support through university for scholars in Scotland from lower-income backgrounds.

Did you always want to work for a charity?

I studied sociology at Glasgow University and was really interested in working with vulnerable groups. But I was quite naïve about the charity world – I thought it was just the household names. I didn't know much about charitable trusts, or the huge number of much smaller charities that they support.

What was your foot in the door?

I actually went through the Trust's bursary programme myself, as I was brought up by my gran when my mum died, and needed financial support to go through university. At that time, I really only knew about the scholarship programme – not the wider work of the Trust. It was only after I graduated that I found out about a six-month paid internship and applied.

What happened next?

I made a role for myself, really. I created and developed it, and made sure they had to keep me on! I started off as an administrative assistant, which was a great way to find out about a lot of different areas of the charity – on any day, I could be helping finance, processing applications or keeping the website running. I really enjoyed that variety and learned a lot. Now I'm helping look after the same bursary programme that I went through as a scholar, which is fantastic.

What's your top tip for charity jobseekers?

Just get as much experience as you can. And don't focus only on the larger charities. Always look for the smaller ones that go under the radar.

Working for an NGO

There are other kinds of organization rooted in ethical values, which typically focus on improving people's lives abroad and are often charities but sometimes not. These are non-governmental organizations, more commonly known as NGOs.

Wikipedia (which is itself part of an NGO) gives the following definition:

'An NGO is an organization that is neither a part of a government nor a conventional for-profit business. Usually set up by ordinary citizens, NGOs may be funded by governments, foundations, businesses, or private persons.'

That only tells you so much – and you'll struggle to find a clearer explanation of an NGO. There are countless variations and interpretations – and many countries have different ideas of what NGOs are really for.

For simplicity, we can say that NGOs are often active in human rights, the environment, health, or community development. (That could be locally, regionally, nationally or internationally.)

While NGOs aren't owned by governments, many of them *do* receive a lot of state funding. For example, the International Red Cross is partially funded by those countries which are signed up to the Geneva Conventions.

Others refuse all state money. Greenpeace, for example, is one of the world's best-known NGOs. It refuses any government funding, as it often needs to hold governments to account on their environmental records.

The Top 10

Let's look at a few examples. Every year, the Global Journal ranks the world's leading 500 NGOs. Here are the Top 10 from 2015:

1. **BRAC** – a Bangladeshi organization working with people whose lives are dominated by extreme poverty, illiteracy, disease and other handicaps.

   brac.net

2. **The Wikimedia Foundation** – dedicated to encouraging the growth and development of free content, multilingual, wiki-based projects.

   wikimediafoundation.org

3. **Acumen Fund** – raising money to invest in companies, leaders and ideas that change the way the world tackles poverty.   acumen.org

4. **Danish Refugee Council** – a humanitarian, non-governmental, non-profit organization helping conflict-affected communities and people.   drc.dk

5. **Partners in Health** – a global health organization committed to improving the health of poor and marginalized people.   pih.org

6. **Ceres** – a national coalition of investors, environmental organizations and other public-interest groups working with companies to address sustainability issues.   ceres.org

7. **CARE International** – fighting poverty and injustice in the world's most vulnerable places.   careinternational.org.uk

8. **Médecins sans Frontières** – a medical humanitarian organization aiding victims of armed conflict, epidemics, and other disasters.   msf.org.uk

9. **Cure Violence** – an innovative NGO aiming to stop the spread of violence in communities by using the methods and strategies associated with disease control.   cureviolence.org

10. **Mercy Corps** – helping people around the world survive and thrive after conflict, crisis and natural disaster.   mercycorps.org.uk

Even people who have worked in the charity sector for many years won't have heard of all of these names – yet they are the global Top 10! There are literally thousands of NGOs operating around the world, and it's important they don't go under your radar.

'I want to help change things'

Robert Johnson
Architect at the UN World Food Programme

What I do now...

I'm working in South Sudan as a facilities architect for the UN. Millions of tonnes of food need to get to emergency situations. I'm designing field and distribution sites and getting them built, as well as air terminals and staff housing.

How I got here...

During my degree, I took a placement year to do voluntary work. That was for a big NGO called Habitat for Humanity, building houses in Ecuador. I just wanted to get my hands dirty – I was halfway through a seven-year architecture degree, and that experience really launched everything.

What happened next?

After graduating, I could have got a job in the Third World as a rookie architect – but I wanted to get good experience and learn the trade in the UK first. I did that for six years, but always knew it wasn't my long-term goal. During that time, I did voluntary work in my holidays – including a trip to Brazil to work with slum communities.

I took the jump...

In 2012, I left the practice and started volunteering full-time for a UK-based NGO. I did some commercial projects on the side to earn money, and spent the rest of the week designing schools and orphanages in Africa. It was a good stepping-stone – I met a lot of contacts, and that led to a job offer.

My motivation...

Initially, it was an adventure – but also about a strong passion for social justice, the idea that there doesn't have to be inequality in the world. I have a lot of gratitude for what I have, and want to use that to help things change – rather than live a comfortable, safe lifestyle at home.

Did I have to make sacrifices?

A lot of architecture is about order and beauty, but when you're building in parts of Africa, many things are ruled out – so you have to compromise. But the sense of purpose more than balances that out.

Voluntary work is...

Golden. It gets you quickly into places, gives you experience and contacts. It was useful for me at different stages along the way – helping me on the next step.

Pursuing a career less ordinary...

Takes a bit of courage, a few leaps of faith and jumping out of your safety net. But it's worth it.

"Just one degree of change can lead to massive impact downstream."

Gib Bullock

Working for a social enterprise

Charities aren't the only organizations that are intrinsically about doing 'good'. If you've ever bought a copy of *The Big Issue*, shopped at the Co-op or visited the Eden Project, you've supported a social enterprise. These are not charities – but they do exist primarily to make a positive difference in the world. Here's a definition from national membership body Social Enterprise UK:

> 'Social enterprises trade to tackle social problems, improve communities, people's life chances, or the environment. They make their money from selling goods and services in the open market, but they reinvest their profits back into the business or the local community. And so, when they profit, society profits.'

How many social enterprises are there in the UK? Some reports say around 70,000 – but there isn't an accurate source for this data.

One reason is that the definition of a social enterprise is quite vague. There's also no social-enterprise version of the Charity Commission, which gives an organization its charitable status. 'Social enterprise' is more like an umbrella term.

Not (always) a charity...

To make things more complicated, some charities actually classify themselves as social enterprises – or they will have a social-enterprise arm, which earns money that is then reinvested into the main charity.

As charities need to become ever more resourceful and entrepreneurial – and look for new ways to find new revenue – this is likely to happen more and more. The lines between charity and social enterprise will become increasingly blurred.

...but not (quite) like a business

Just as charities are becoming more business-like, so traditional businesses are thinking harder about their environmental and social impact – and wanting to do something about it.

We'll look at the best examples in the next chapter (The Changers). But again, some appear to be squeezing into the social-enterprise space. And, given that some social enterprises are structured as limited companies, it can be hard to tell them apart.

The social-enterprise difference

The easiest way to understand how social enterprises are different from 'business as usual' is to focus on what happens to the money made.

Social enterprises offer services or trade (often in specifically 'ethical' areas, for example, organic food or sustainably sourced clothing), they make money, and they pay salaries to their directors and employees.

The big difference between them and a highly principled company (which has a great social and environmental policy) is that social enterprises don't pay any profits or dividends to their shareholders.

Instead, they reinvest all their surpluses – and 'do good' with this profit, whether that's supporting a particular charity, or reinvesting it in the social enterprise.

HOW IT USED TO BE:

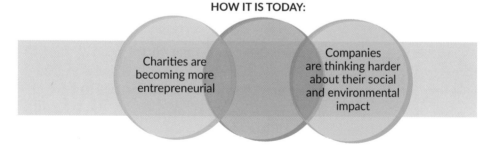

	Charity	**Social Enterprise**	**Traditional Business**
Mission:	Only to help others	Profit, social and environmental	Profit only
Financial model:	Donations only	Trade to help others	Make money for shareholders

HOW IT IS TODAY:

Charities are becoming more entrepreneurial

Companies are thinking harder about their social and environmental impact

Why work for a social enterprise?

One of the advantages of working for a social enterprise – rather than a charity – is that you can feel more in control.

Although some charities are very bold, the majority rely very heavily on grant funding and this can affect the way they work.

For example, charities can become understandably preoccupied with pleasing their grant-makers. And, even when they get the money, many grants come with strings attached. This means charities can't always spend the money as they would like.

It can all result in a feeling of powerlessness – that the charity isn't in control of its own destiny – and that can affect people working in the organization.

Though some social enterprises are able to access grants, they typically rely far less on donations and fundraising. Instead, they tend to behave much more like an entrepreneurial, traditional business – only with social and environmental concerns at its core.

Even if the pressure is on to make money, this can create a brilliant sense of team spirit. As an employee, you will have opportunities to help the organization become more successful and profitable – knowing that any surplus money will be spent on good causes.

Which social enterprise?

There are a number of ways to run a social enterprise. If you're interesting in working in the sector, it's worth knowing a little more about them – so you can see which might be most aligned with your values.

Although some social enterprises are structured no differently from a regular business, there are three legal structures specifically designed for social enterprises:

- Community Interest Companies (CICs)
- Co-operatives
- Industrial & Provident Societies (IPSs).

Searching for these can be a great shortcut to an ethically aligned employer.

Community Interest Companies

More commonly known as CICs (pronounced 'kicks'), this kind of social enterprise has only been in existence for about 10 years.

One of the reasons it was created was to give ethically minded entrepreneurs a special legal status that would give them the best bits of private business, without losing sight of their ethical purpose.

There are some great reasons for being a charity (including qualifying for grants and tax relief), but it can be restrictive and involve a lot of bureaucracy – and many socially minded entrepreneurs wanted more freedom.

Previously, many had ended up creating regular private companies, and simply choosing to reinvest in the community. The CIC enabled them to have a distinctive legal form that *proved* they were walking the talk.

One of the most important features of a CIC is something called an 'asset lock', which means that company profits cannot simply be paid out to shareholders: the majority has to be retained for community benefit. Unlike a regular business, company owners also cannot 'cash in' when they sell the business. In other words, any profit automatically goes back to the community.

That aside, a CIC is similar to a regular business – so it gives people a lot of freedom to make business decisions quickly and generate as much revenue as possible, doing good along the way.

Today, there are over 10,000 CICs in the UK and roughly 1 in every 200 new companies created is a CIC. They are as varied as the charity sector – and can range from small 'kitchen table' type outfits, to multi-million-pound turnover organizations employing thousands of people.

> Profits cannot simply be paid out to shareholders: the majority has to be retained for community benefit.

'This is incredibly rewarding'

Rinal Pandya

Employer engagement manager at Women Like Us

Have you always worked for a social enterprise?

No, I worked in the private sector for many years, and built up experience in sales and online advertising. When I moved into recruitment, I also started on the commercial side. I was a sales manager for the private company Timewise, which helps fund Women Like Us.

What was your turning point?

When I went on maternity leave. I immediately realized the problems that many women have when they want to go back to work afterwards. I couldn't commit to a regular 9-to-5 job, there were lots of childcare complications and the commute became a real problem. As a parent, you need flexibility.

What happened next?

I moved across to Women Like Us, which is a social enterprise that helps women with children find work that fits with their lives. I support parents directly by helping them find opportunities.

Are you using the same skills?

Yes, I still use my sales and negotiation skills every day. After all, it's still the bottom dollar that counts for businesses – so I work hard to outline the business benefits of hiring our applicants.

Do you feel like you're making a positive difference?

Definitely. The effect is incredible. You can really see people's confidence grow. A lot of parents may settle for roles that are actually below them; they certainly don't punch above their weight. For example, we've seen successful finance professionals who've taken jobs in supermarkets after maternity leave. We have helped people like that get back to where they should be.

Could you go back to a corporate role?

No. This is incredibly rewarding – and I wouldn't be getting up every day to do it if I didn't feel like that. Financially, I don't earn as much as I could in a purely private job, but I get much more out of it. I think my priorities have changed, though. Ten years ago, I wouldn't have felt the same – but as a mum, it's different. As long as the bills are paid, it's not just about the money.

Community business

City Health Care Partnership CIC is a remarkable social business. It currently provides a wide range of health and care services to over half a million local people in Hull, the East Riding of Yorkshire and Knowsley, Merseyside. It employs approximately 1,500 people.

The CIC helps to minimize the need for acute care in hospital – through early interventions, community-based treatment and promotion of healthy lifestyles. As well as managing over 75 different services – from school nurses to prison health – it also runs a retail, care-home and wholesale-pharmacy business.

Describing itself as 'a co-owned for better profit business', City Health invests all profits into services, staff and the communities in which it works. Its 2015 Social Return on Investment audit showed a return of £33 for every £1 spent.

chcpcic.org.uk

Co-operatives

You've probably shopped at a Co-op, but how much do you know about co-operatives?

Unlike CICs, they have been around for a long time. It's more than 250 years since a group of weavers in Scotland formed arguably the first co-operative of the industrial age. Today, Rochdale is known worldwide as the birthplace of the modern co-operative movement. By setting up a co-operative society in 1844, the 'Rochdale Pioneers' popularized the concept of giving profits to members based on the purchases they make. (This was known as the 'divi'.)

Today, there are many different kinds of co-operatives, but they all share a common characteristic. Each one is a group of people, acting together, and meeting the common needs and aims of members. They share ownership and make decisions democratically. Essentially, they are businesses run for the people by the people.

There are now over 6,000 co-operative businesses in the UK, contributing over £37 billion to the economy. There are more member owners of co-ops (just over 15 million) than there are direct shareholders of businesses in the UK.

So, co-ops are a big deal, and a huge employer. And by far the UK's biggest co-op is The Co-operative Group, which currently has 70,000 staff in the UK.

Though its banking division almost collapsed in 2013, the Co-op has many other profitable businesses, such as food, funeral care, legal services and electricals. Its eight million members are involved in the group's business strategy – deciding how its social goals are achieved and who shares in its profits.

The Co-op has also long been known as an ethical retailer. As well as sharing profits with staff and members, it was the first UK retailer to champion fair trade, invests a huge amount of money into community projects and renewable energy, and has won many awards for seeking to improve animal-welfare standards.

Which co-op?

There are four different kinds of co-operative ownership:

Consumer-owned: Where the members are the customers of the co-operative. This could mean they purchase food from a consumer retail society like Central England Co-operative, have an account with a credit union or are a resident in a housing co-operative.

Worker-owned: Where the members work in the co-operative. This could be directly as owners, as in the case of a worker co-operative like Dulas, or indirectly through a beneficiary trust like John Lewis, as long as there is a representative link back to the workforce.

Enterprise-owned: Where the members are businesses that trade with the co-operative. This could be supplying produce as a farmer, purchasing supplies as an independent retailer or sharing services like a taxi driver or market trader.

Mixed ownership: Where the members are a mix of the above but they all share a specific community of interest. This could be that they all support the same football club, want to save their local pub or to run a village shop.

In focus: Suma Wholefoods
suma.coop

Businesses of all types have in recent years been striving to 'engage' their employees. Suma Wholefoods, a Yorkshire-based wholefoods distributor, has been succeeding at this for decades. A worker co-operative with 140 owners, no hierarchy and equal pay, it turns over £34 million a year.

Its sales have doubled in the last 10 years, and in 2013 it paid a bonus of £4,750 to every employee. Suma's secret? Giving people ownership of the business and rewarding them for their work. As Bob Cannell, a Suma member, puts it: 'Our 140 workers are multi-skilled, rotating between jobs as required, and we manage the business co-operatively. Everyone is paid an equal wage. When everyone benefits, everyone works hard for success.'

Source: Co-operatives UK

'It does feel like a family'

Lorna Macdonald

Human resources manager at the Edinburgh Bicycle Co-operative

How did you start out?

I did an Arts degree in Politics and Sociology, and wasn't sure what to do afterwards. I went travelling and took a few jobs (some very interesting, some less so) and eventually ended up at a big American company which was full of corporate speak. I think it was when we had a meeting to discuss how we could cut down our meetings that I finally knew I couldn't stand it!

How did you begin in the Co-op?

I started part-time in an admin role. I immediately felt it was more 'me' – the people were very relaxed and friendly, and although there was a hierarchical structure it still felt like the complete opposite from the big corporate giants. The Co-op progressed quickly – and as we grew, we needed to get a bit more professional. I'd been involved in aspects of Human Resources [HR] from the start, and I was lucky enough that the Bike Co-op supported me to obtain a formal qualification [in HR] as I was working.

What's the best thing about working for a co-op?

One part is transparency. Even the Saturday person who may work one day a month gets to see all the financial info and has the opportunity to input – it's all out in the open. People often don't appreciate this until they work elsewhere. There's also a quirky side to the business – and even though we've grown, there's still a sense of humour about the business. It's generally a really good bunch of people working here.

And the worst?

There are challenges when you get bigger – growing pains. Not all of our members wanted the business to go the way it has done, and that can result in some animosity. With the co-op model, some people do feel a sense of entitlement and are more interested in their rights than the responsibilities that go alongside that. I think people can expect too much from a co-op – for some people, it's a way of life rather than just a job, which can be fantastic but can also lead to unrealistic expectations that can't always be met. Also, it's worth remembering that people are people – and much as we'd like to think that working co-operatively might result in folk behaving better at work that's not always the case!

Which kinds of people suit a co-op?

It's funny – we do generally attract a lot of people who are anti-corporate, people who've hated working for the bank! Even if people could probably earn a bit more elsewhere, there's something about the fabric of a co-op that draws people in. It does feel like a family, even if it's a bit dysfunctional sometimes!

What qualities should they have?

I think people who are self-starters are a good fit. We don't have layers of support that people may be used to in other businesses. In a corporation you may have multiple levels of seniority above you. Here, it's your responsibility – people are expected to self-manage, you have a lot more independence and need to go away and find things out for yourself.

Do the ethics of the co-op still motivate you?

Yes, they're really important. I could never go to work in HR at somewhere that treats people really shabbily. I think we do things the right way – and when I see how other employers treat people, I just couldn't do that.

edinburghbicycle.com

The IPS files

Co-operatives are an interesting kind of business. They can't be charities, they can sometimes be CICs, but most of the time they are legally structured in one of two ways: either as a regular limited company, or an industrial and provident society (IPS).

This isn't a book about corporate legal structures. But if you're interested in pursuing a career in social enterprise, it is worth knowing that there are two different kinds of IPS: co-operatives and community benefit societies (often called 'ben comms').

They're very similar but one of the main differences is that 'ben comms' are run for the benefit of the *community* at large – rather than just for members of the society. (Both kinds of IPS are registered with the Financial Conduct Authority.)

To add a bit more complexity, they both fall under yet another grouping, known as 'Mutuals', which also include credit unions and building societies.

You'll find many of these are in the banking or insurance sector. If you're interested in finance, or increasing financial fairness – for example, helping economically disadvantaged communities in the UK – exploring the world of Mutuals could be a very useful starting point.

The Mutuals Public Register web search isn't very user-friendly, but it's a trusted place to find registered credit unions, IPS, co-operatives and other kinds of mutual organization.   mutuals.fsa.gov.uk/Search.aspx

Which jobs are out there?

What kinds of roles exist in the charity and social-enterprise sector? The answer is almost limitless. With over 160,000 charities in the UK alone, there is a vast range of causes that you can support.

If you have a clear passion – for example, equality in the workplace – this can help you target exactly the right positions. You'll have fewer options but at least you can focus your energies on only the most relevant organizations.

But if you don't have one clear direction, that's okay too. In practice, the charity sector is incredibly fluid – and people often move between very different kinds of organization.

For example, you'll often see people moving from a children's charity to an environmental group. For them, the most important point is supporting something worthwhile, rather than being tied to a particular cause. The good news is that HR teams see any charity experience as a big plus.

> **If you have a clear passion this can help you target exactly the right positions.**

Top purposes

If you look at the job market for charities and social enterprises, you can quickly start to group the kinds of organizations into different areas. The visual spread on the next two pages displays the vast range of areas that such organizations embrace. This list isn't definitive, and there's a great deal of crossover between all these types of mission that you could be supporting.

The most common charity career themes

Advice
– empowering and aiding people in need.
Example:
Citizens Advice

Advocacy
– fighting for changes to policy and law.
Example: International Justice Mission

Animal
– protecting animals in need.
Example: RSPCA

Arts, culture and education
– from heritage and museums, to creativity and learning.
Example: National Trust

Children
– support for young people, from mental and physical health to rights and opportunities.
Example: Young Minds

Community development
– helping economically, socially and financially disadvantaged people.
Example: Oxfam

Crime
– justice and crime prevention to rehabilitation:
Example: Reprieve

Disability
– working for people with mental and physical disabilities.
Example: Scope

Environment
– biodiversity and habitat protection to green technology.
Example:
Friends of the Earth

Equality
- campaigning and action for vulnerable or marginalized groups
Example: End Violence Against Women

Faith-based
- charities founded in the values of a particular religious belief.
Example: Jewish Care

Housing and homelessness
- helping people get off the street.
Example: Shelter

Health
- research and disease prevention to healthy living and medical care.
Example: Macmillan Cancer Support

Human rights
- defending and extending people's rights and freedoms.
Example: Liberty

Mental Health
- supporting people with mental-health problems.
Example: MIND

Policy and research
- think tanks and research institutes.
Example: The Joseph Rowntree Foundation

International
- providing aid, care and support abroad.
Example: Care International

Poverty relief
- preventing and ending world poverty.
Example: Comic Relief

Social welfare
- looking after the wellbeing of an entire society.
Example: Turn2Us

Your skills

Charities are always rooted in one of 13 core purposes (see Page 40), but the charity and social-enterprise sectors need a vast range of skills. There's no reason why you can't combine what you're good at – and what you love – with an ethical career.

If you already know what you want to learn or how to apply your skills – for example, as a teacher, web developer or an engineer – this will help you narrow down the options.

You may also find specific websites and resources just for your area. For example, Adventure Medic is a great place to find international nursing and medical jobs with humanitarian organizations: go to **theadventuremedic.com/jobs/**

If you haven't decided what to focus on yet, or don't have a specialism, there are still many entry routes. The skills of a generalist – someone who can successfully jump between skillsets – are especially useful in the charity and social-enterprise sector, where people need to take on many different roles, learn on the job and be open to overcoming new challenges.

Most popular jobs

It is perhaps no surprise that the charity sector seems rather obsessed with money. As no-one is making a profit and most charities rely heavily on donations to survive, generating revenue is a huge priority – and this affects the job opportunities available.

The website **charityjob.co.uk** is one of the UK's most popular specialist charity job websites – typically featuring over 4,000 current vacancies for 900+ different charities.

On a typical day, you'll find that the most frequently posted charity jobs tend to be (in order):

1. Fundraising (usually twice as many as any other category)

2. Support worker

3. Finance

4. Social Care/Development

5. Management

6. Admin

7. Marketing

8. Social work

9. Communications/PR

10. Project management

Some of the other most popular charity job categories include:

- Advocacy
- Business development
- Campaigning
- Digital
- Human resources
- IT
- Legal
- Nursing
- Policy/research
- Teaching

Beyond the norm

If you don't see your skills here, don't worry. These are only the most common kinds of jobs.

The charity and social-enterprise sector is incredibly diverse, and you will be able to find job opportunities across a wide range of areas. Remember that there are many interesting third-sector jobs that you may not even realize exist.

'I'm in a niche role, but I absolutely love it'

Paul Weaver
Digital Innovations Manager,
Cancer Research

How did you start out?

I studied Industrial Design at university. Then I got onto a graduate scheme with Apple, really to broaden my horizons and get experience of big organizations.

Was it good?

Those two years were exceptionally good for my development. There was a lot of one-on-one time with smart people, and I learned a lot. But I also knew it wasn't for me. I've always been keen to work on things that have a big impact – but I didn't just want to make someone else rich or keep shareholders happy. I wanted to explore what was out there.

What happened next?

I'd heard about innovation jobs in general from Apple – and then I found out that Cancer Research had a dedicated innovation team. They were solely focused on generating new ideas around income streams for the charity. What's the next way of communicating with people and raising money?

What kind of thing did you do?

We'd get a challenge from the Board – say to increase the number of young men supporting the charity, and we'd go away, research and generate new ideas.

We'd then pilot them and see what worked. For example, with young men we came up with the Dryathlon – giving up alcohol for a month for charity – and that's now in its third year.

What do you do now?

I've since moved into the digital team at Cancer Research – and I'm looking at innovation purely from a digital perspective. That means looking at the world, identifying the biggest trends, and picking out what's relevant. For example, we're looking at virtual reality and have done a lot of work around contactless payments. I'm in a very niche role, but I absolutely love it.

What kind of recruit are you after?

When we recruit, the most important thing is if they're an interesting person. When I started, there were 12 of us and we all had very different backgrounds – one of the bosses had been a sailing instructor! It's about bringing a new way of working to the team, having the confidence to get involved, to tackle things that aren't black and white, and be able to jump in without always knowing the full picture.

cancerresearchuk.org

Small or big?

*Charity media manager **Fiona Furman** has worked in the third sector for over 20 years. Here are her top tips on deciding whether to work for a big or a small charity.*

I've worked on both sides – from large organizations like MND Association and World Vision to a small (but global) charity like Toybox, which works to support street children across the world. Both can be very rewarding; it depends on where you're at and how you like to work.

If you're the kind of person who likes to have an idea and make it happen quickly, you might find that smaller charities will be right for you. It's that much easier to experiment and get on with a job.

Bigger charities are larger beasts and they can be a lot slower. You can find that you need to have multiple meetings to get anything done. But if you enjoy planning, developing ideas and really getting into the detail, there's more structure and process with bigger charities. And you can be involved in some brilliant work.

Remember that, because bigger charities have more staff, there's a greater likelihood that you'll need to specialize. They're looking for you to be (or become) an expert in one aspect of work.

This can be a good thing, but I've found that being asked to do a much broader sweep of work can enable you to find what you're good at. That's what happened to me, and it's a really helpful way to formulate your career.

How do you find a doer job?

You now know more about the charity and social enterprise sector, and the kinds of roles available. But how do you find the jobs?

The first step is to do your research. If you've read through Chapter 2, you'll already have spent some time thinking about the kind of role and organization you want to work in, and created a charity shortlist. This will help you focus your research, and show you have a plan, for example, if you speak to recruitment agencies.

There are four popular – and successful – routes for finding out about job opportunities: the media; going direct; agencies; and social media.

1 Media

Check the press for charity job adverts – the *Guardian* charity job microsite is an excellent place to find opportunities. There is also a range of specialist charity media sites and national newspapers, which regularly advertise new opportunities. Remember that smaller charities won't typically have the budgets to advertise their roles in the nationals, or through recruitment agencies – so local papers and magazines may offer roles that aren't shown elsewhere.

2 Go direct

Most charities have their own websites – and they will almost always feature new positions there. In some cases, this may be the only place they publish new vacancies – as it doesn't cost them anything to advertise. Check the websites of your charity and social-enterprise shortlist regularly, and sign up for job 'alerts' if they offer them. Even if an organization isn't offering a position right now, you can always get in touch and see if they might need your skills. (See right, 'Hidden jobs'.)

Remember that smaller charities will often be more open to generalists who have a wide range of skills and interests. For example, the marketing person may be responsible for everything from creating press releases to designing leaflets, updating the website and writing social-media posts. In general, bigger charities tend to want specialists, who can prove they're able to do exactly what the role demands.

3 Agencies

When you factor in their commission, recruitment agencies can take a reasonable amount of your wages. But if you're finding it hard to get in front of employers, they can be a great option. There are a growing number of specialist recruitment agencies for charity jobs. These can be especially useful, as they work with charities every day and understand how best to sell in your skills and experience. If you're new to the sector, they may also be able to advise you on the best way to get charity job-ready.

Don't ignore the mainstream recruitment agencies, though. They will also have a number of charity jobs on their books, and – if you're looking for a specialist role – they may have opportunities that the general charity recruitment agencies don't know about.

For example, a larger charity with a specialist financial role may use an agency that focuses only on financial recruitment.

Hidden jobs

Some recruitment websites say that 70 per cent of jobs are never advertised. There's no reliable evidence for this statistic, but it's clear that many charity roles are never publicized.

This means it's often a good idea to contact charities speculatively. You'll have less competition if the job isn't advertised. And if you come with a recommendation, you may well be given a chance to prove yourself.

> Specialist recruitment agencies for charity jobs understand how best to sell in your skills and experience.

4 Social networks

Many charities increasingly use social media as a free and effective way to spread the word about job vacancies. Make sure you follow your shortlist organizations on social media – especially on Twitter – to keep up-to-date.

Non-recruitment specific charity networks – such as an informal Facebook group for charity professionals – are also excellent places to hear about new opportunities, sometimes before they're formally advertised (see more on Page 71 – 'How to get job-ready'.)

The Jobs section of LinkedIn is a superb resource. You can filter by multiple job criteria (including 'Non-profit' as an industry type), and create job alerts for regular, automatic job updates. You can also see if you can connect to someone at an organization that's advertising a role, and ask for a referral or just some advice.

Many organizations, especially smaller ones, have good reasons for keeping things quiet. Advertising jobs is expensive, and they may have to sort through hundreds of CVs and application forms.

Finding the perfect charity job

*Neil Hogan, deputy MD of Charity People,
shares his top tips.*

The one thing I always tell people...
is to find out what floats their boat. What
are the kinds of charities that motivate
them most? It could be one area or many
– and that's great, as their pool gets a bit
wider. If the cause matters to them, they'll
be more passionate about their job.

My top tips for finding a great charity job:

Get organized: Create an Excel sheet and list 50-100 of your ideal charities in
one column. Add in a link to all of their job pages, and get signed up to their
job alerts where possible. You can use keywords to make sure you only get
the most relevant ones: for example, 'graduate' or 'junior' or a certain salary
range.

Walk the talk: Volunteering is a great way to meet some people who are
part of these organizations. You'll find out more about what it's like to work
there, how you might fit, and get your face known. The same is true of
fundraising. If you can say in an interview that you ran a marathon for the
charity and raised £500, that will push you further ahead.

Connect online: Start to create your own network on LinkedIn. Create a
profile and make it look professional. (Remember to use an email address
that doesn't sound daft!) Look back at your 50-100 charities, find them on
LinkedIn and look at the people who work there. You can start to build your
network from here. It's a smart way to increase your exposure and potential
to be headhunted – as charities' hiring managers always like to recruit
people directly. charitypeople.co.uk

How to make recruitment agencies work for you

*Want to get the most out of your experience with a recruitment agency? **Julian Smith** from ethical job and networking agency, I AM Enterprises, explains how.*

As a candidate, you may not be paying a fee for a service, but you hold a lot of the power. Without you, a recruiter won't get paid.

He or she can have the best vacancies in the world, but without the perfect candidates, this means absolutely nothing. At the end of the day, my advice is to make the most out of the recruiter; make him or her work for you. Here's how:

What else do they have? I always explain to my candidates that if I have 50 suitable roles, they can go forward for all 50. We want to secure a fee, yes, but we also want a happy candidate, since they'll be our marketing going forward – and a happy candidate is one who feels that the recruiter always acts with their best interests at heart.

Research an organization: What is the agent's relationship with an organization? Have they worked together for a long time? If so, what is their track record of placing candidates with them, and who can you talk to so as to get a more informed 'feel' for the organization? Can the agent get you supplementary documents, such as strategic plans or annual accounts?

Interview preparation: Who will be interviewing you, and what does the recruiter know about them? What is the format of the interview? Has the recruiter been to the offices before, and what is the best way to get there? Are there any tests and, if so, what are they likely to cover?

Interview practice: Haven't been interviewed for a while? Not a problem – ask for interview practice, or a mock interview with your consultant. If they claim to be too busy, remind them that you will be making them a nice fee...

The go-between: If you get offered the role, talk to the consultant about any concerns you have – and let them negotiate on your behalf. A good recruiter will be able to do this – and an ethical recruiter will be very open and honest, brokering a deal which leaves both sides feeling that they have 'won'.

iamenterprises.co.uk

The jobseeker view...

Marie Curie's social-media manager, Marie Faulkner (interviewed on Page 79), used a recruitment agency when she began looking to break into the voluntary sector. Here are her Top Five tips:

- **Take the positives – and share your enthusiasm**. Being able to talk to and get feedback from recruitment consultants actually gave me a little hope – something you very, very rarely get applying for jobs online. I was finally given the chance to show off my enthusiasm and personality to an adviser who could then vouch for me for any upcoming opportunities.

- **Keep improving your CV**. After telling the agency what I wanted and what experience I have, they helped me realize what the strengths and weaknesses of my CV were. They helped me de-clutter it by telling me to separate each job into responsibilities and achievements. They also suggested using a small paragraph at the beginning of my CV to really cater to each job I was applying for.

- **Get interview insights.** My recruitment agency also shared their knowledge and experience of the current job climate; in my case it was the demand for social-media skills. And before an interview they can really help you with questions about the prospective employer, what they're looking for and sometimes even how the interview went for other candidates.

- **Keep talking.** Maintain a good relationship with your consultant. I did this by checking in with them throughout my job search and temporary placements. I was always honest with my consultant about what I wanted, how placements were going and any jobs that I was going for on my own.

- **Take your chances.** While you are finding work, make the most of your time. Try to get as much training and as many new skills as possible, establish new relationships in the sector of your choice and really think about what you want to do. If it's a temporary placement they may keep you on. If not, make sure you get a really good reference.

"
There is no point in work unless it absorbs you like an absorbing game.
"

DH Lawrence

How to get job-ready for the charity sector

It's all very well knowing where to find charity and social-enterprise jobs. But how do you make sure that you're best prepared to impress the interviewers?

1 Volunteer

Ask anyone working at a charity about how to get into the sector, and you'll almost always hear the 'v' word: volunteering.

Curiously, it seems that giving your time for nothing can actually lead to some great paid opportunities. Not only will you pick up new skills and experiences, but volunteering also underlines your commitment and dedication. Often, it may not matter which charity you've helped, as long as you show you've volunteered for an organization.

Volunteering shows that you care about certain issues, that you're 'walking the talk' and looking to make a positive difference. But it's good to remember that not all volunteering is the same.

Some people volunteer for a short while before being offered a job. Others may volunteer for many different organizations, but feel no closer to getting permanent employment. There can be a financial implications to giving away your time (especially in the working week) – and many people simply cannot afford to volunteer for a charity without a clear idea of where this investment of time will take them.

As this is such an increasingly important area, there is a whole chapter in this book on volunteering. The aim is to help you find interesting volunteering opportunities, and to use your time effectively – so that you can look back on your volunteering as a valuable step on the way to your chosen career.

2 Build an online brand

What would a charity's HR manager find if they searched your name online? What impression would you make if they found your social-media accounts?

Many employers and recruiters will search for your name when they receive an application or CV – and you want to stand out for the right reasons.

Building a professional presence online can be a brilliant way to kick-start your charity career. If you do it right, you can connect with the right people, prove your commitment to the causes that matter to you, and show off your experience, skills and knowledge.

It's not just about finding a job today. This is both a short- and long-term investment, as you can continue to add your professional experiences as you progress your career – building a strong 'brand' online, and helping you stand out from the crowd.

Start connecting

Social enterprises and charities see themselves as very different from 'business as usual', and – if you want to break into them – it's a good idea to start connecting with people who are active in those worlds. They can be surprisingly small circles – and you never know how a contact or familiar name can help your career search.

There are a number of ways to grow your profile successfully online:

- **Charity and social-enterprise groups** There are lots of informal online groups for charities – from sector-wide forums (such as the very popular 'Charity UK' group on LinkedIn) to cause-related social groups (such as environmental campaigns) and role-based social networks (like those for marketing professionals). It's a brilliant way to discover and hear from people who have already found roles in the third sector, and to learn more about charity careers. Start by listening – identify the people who would be useful to have in your network, and gradually begin to contribute.

- **Twitter** Start following the Twitter accounts of every organization on your shortlist. If you're already on Twitter, you may want to create a separate account for this kind of 'professional' following and tweeting. This way, your timeline will look more impressive to anyone who views your profile. As well as building up a strong network, you'll also find that many charity jobs are shared across people's individual social channels. Remember to jump into conversations – ask questions, comment, and 'like' the posts and updates that spark your enthusiasm or imagination.

- **LinkedIn** The world's largest professional social network has become a vital tool for any jobseeker. From first-time charity jobbers to chief executives, it is used by almost everyone. (This includes professional charity job recruiters, who increasingly use LinkedIn to headhunt staff for their clients.)

  Do you have a professional-looking LinkedIn page? Ideally, it should clearly state your career ambitions, values and any relevant experience, especially volunteering. Always put yourself in the shoes of a potential employer or recruiter – what would they think if they saw your profile?

  When you're happy, the next step is to start connecting through LinkedIn with people who can help you further your career. As well as finding and responding to interesting posts (as on Twitter), LinkedIn makes it easy to find and connect directly with potentially valuable connections – searching by role and/or organization.

- **Personal websites** Creating a professional-looking personal website has become very cheap and simple. It is a great way to keep your personal information up-to-date and accessible to the world. You can point people here to find your online CV, show your passions and previous experience, present any work examples on a portfolio page, and add any supportive testimonial quotes.

  If you have a particular interest area, you could also have a blog on your website – where you write, comment on or curate topics that are relevant.

  Away from your site, don't forget to comment on other people's blogs to raise your visibility. To make sure you're using your time effectively, it's important to filter out the unhelpful 'noise' on social media and identify popular bloggers and organizations that can help you get noticed.

> **Tip**
>
> Make sure your personal Facebook account has the privacy setting switched on – so potential employers cannot see your personal photos and updates.

3 Take it offline

Thinking digitally is a brilliant way to find an ethical career – but sometimes the smartest thing to do is go offline.

The UK charity sector has a very busy and popular calendar of events throughout the year. This is most active in major cities – and heavily skewed towards London – so your options will be more limited if you're in an area without much of a charity scene. But if you're within striking distance of the capital, there are many opportunities to get out there and meet people who are working in the third sector. Many of these networking events are free and some are designed specifically for newcomers.

As well as social meet-ups, training and development events are also excellent ways to meet like-minded people and gain some new skills. The Institute of Fundraising, for example, has a range of short professional courses that can help you get to grips with the basics, or specialize in a specific area of work.

4 Find a mentor

Many seasoned charity and social-enterprise professionals are happy to share their experiences either formally or informally – and you could benefit from their advice and connections.

That's just what Tessa Cooper did before she joined the massive open online course (MOOC) learning platform, FutureLearn.

'Don't let youth be a barrier'

Tessa Cooper
Product Manager, FutureLearn

How did you find your first mentor?

I didn't specifically go out to find a mentor – it was just a natural thing that happened. It started when I was working in admin at *The Guardian*. As part of the job I had to chat to a lot of people. I started asking them to have a cup of tea with me so I could find out more about their jobs.

With a lot of people I struggled to think about what I was going to say. I didn't feel I was very good at networking but I realized that – with just a couple of questions and a cuppa

– people would happily talk for ages about what they do, and I could learn from them.

I began telling people I liked, or who were doing interesting things, that I'd be happy to help them out, even in my spare time. It was the head of professional networks at the paper who first gave me a chance to help out running some events. And by doing that on a more formal basis, it landed me a job in the marketing team.

They realized it was better to trust me with more responsibilities than to hire someone new. They also liked helping out young, lower-salaried, people to progress their careers.

Did networking lead to other opportunities?

After about three years at *The Guardian* I found out about an interview for a project manager job at Bauer Media. My interviewer didn't think I was right for that job but she did offer to meet up for a coffee later. We talked about product management – something I had no idea was a job at the time.

She knew someone in the relevant team and suggested I ask for a secondment as junior product manager. Once I'd got my head around what a product manager did, I was keen to do it as a full-time job, so I applied to FutureLearn. They realized that my passion and working experience were a bonus to the team.

By then, the lady who first interviewed me at Bauer Media had moved on to work at Comic Relief. She got in touch to ask if I'd like to help her team transform their digital strategy. She's someone I look up to and I thought I could learn a lot from working with her, so I went.

What was different about Comic Relief?

It really opened my eyes to what charities can be like. FutureLearn is all about doing something worthwhile – but it's different with Comic Relief. Your driving motivation is to make money for

the organization to survive.

It's very different from many charities because they have a big brand and generate millions of pounds a year. But, because of the way their funding cycles and project grants work, many people working at Comic Relief don't get to see the outcome of their work. I ended up finding that frustrating, so I came back to FutureLearn.

What's your top mentoring advice?

There are two great pieces of advice I've picked up from my mentors over the years:

First, I'd panic a lot when people gave me any tasks that came with a lot of responsibility. My boss at the time asked me, 'What's the worst that could happen? If you get fired, you can find another job. It wouldn't be that bad. You'll rarely get fired for speaking your mind, so take every opportunity to do just that.'

It sounds simple, but that gave me so much confidence. It also gave me the mind-set to go up and talk to interesting people at a company. I realized that 'the worst that could happen' would be that they wouldn't want to talk to me.

The second thing is to not let youth be a barrier. I started my career at 18 and a lot of people have been quite shocked by my age – until quite recently. But by my early 20s, I'd already done a lot in the working world, and I was keen to take on more. It doesn't matter how old you are, show that you're eager and don't be afraid to ask people about their jobs and experiences. Everyone is always learning.

5 Internships

If you're looking to get your first experience of working in the charity world, have you thought about an internship? Many organizations run work-placement schemes, where you can gain valuable on-the-job skills over a fixed period of time.

In particular, internships can be excellent ways to take advantage of valuable charity induction sessions and supervision, benefit from internal training and development courses, and get access to internal job vacancy lists. You may also receive official recognition (e.g. a certificate) following your internship, and a professional reference for your CV. You could even get a job offer.

If you're thinking about interning, it's important to do your research. In the private sector, it is now illegal to hire interns to do work without paying them – unless they're work shadowing or joining as part of a short student placement. But in the charity sector, there's a loophole, where organizations can classify interns as 'voluntary workers' – which means they're not legally required to pay anything.

This is a hot topic – and many people understandably feel very strongly that working interns should *always* be paid.

What does a good internship involve?

In 2013, the organizations Public World and Impact Hub King's Cross ran a 'Fair Trade Internships' workshop with numerous charities, NGOs and social enterprises on the ethics of internships. Together, they decided that charity internships should ideally deliver 10 outcomes:

1. Fairness and respect from the boss and fellow workers.

2. Payment.

3. Duty of care. Employers have a duty of care to their employees, which means that they should take all steps which are reasonably possible to ensure their health, safety and wellbeing.

4. Responsibility to lead a project or to be part of a project.

5. Being able to use an internship as proof that someone is able to work in an English-speaking environment.

6. Applying skills and learning how to work in a business environment.

7. Getting to know another area of work and gaining insights there.

8. A job offer after the internship.

9. Connections and valuable networks.

10. A name on the CV.

You can find out more about Fair Trade Internships at: publicworld.org/projects/

Another good resource here is Intern Aware. As well as offering support and a whistleblowing line for people to report unethical internships, the 'Learn More' section of its website has lots of good advice on how to spot a good (and bad) internship opportunity. Find out more at internaware.org

6 Education and training

What do you need to study to land your dream charity career? Depending on your next move, it could involve several years in academia – or absolutely nothing.

Some charity careers do require very specific qualifications, such as a postgraduate qualification in a particular area of work. Others will give you much more flexibility to learn on the job. We can't list every educational option here – as the list is almost limitless, and will always depend on your career choices and the skills you need.

It is important, though, to note that formal academic learning can be an incredibly useful step on your ethical career ladder. Whether it means enrolling in a short course to boost a particular skill that you know you'll need, or taking a Masters degree to help establish yourself as a specialist in a particular field, there are countless advantages to 'up-skilling' – as many of the people you'll meet in this book can testify.

Although education and training are very individual choices, there are a few institutions that deserve special mention. In the corporate world, the 'MBA' has been seen traditionally as the educational standard for future business leaders – but you would typically struggle to find anything very 'ethical' about the curriculum. In recent years, things have changed, thanks to some pioneering institutions that are putting social entrepreneurship at the heart of its postgraduate programmes.

The **Cass Business School** in London is one example – enabling its MBA students to learn how to weave social and environmental values into successful business leadership. There are lots more courses on offer too. From an MSc in 'Charity Fundraising and Marketing' to a postgraduate diploma in 'Grantmaking, Philanthropy and Social Investment', you can find many ways to gain specific charity and social enterprise-sector qualifications: cass.city.ac.uk

The **Saïd Business School** at Oxford University is another pioneering institution that helps its students become successful social entrepreneurs. Its highly acclaimed MBA programme is designed around the concept of responsible business, and the 'ethical decision-making of business leaders': sbs.ox.ac.uk

In 2003, Saïd launched the **Skoll Centre for Social Entrepreneurship** with 'a mandate to change the world' by investing in the next generation of social entrepreneurs. Among its many initiatives is the Skoll Scholarship, which offers full tuition and a living stipend to join its Oxford MBA programme. This is aimed at individuals committed to 'solving a social or environmental issue and finding entrepreneurial ways of doing so', either by starting a venture or initiative, or by way of a 'portfolio career'. Find out more at: sbs.ox.ac.uk/faculty-research/skoll

No degree, no problem?

Some organizations will only consider graduates for certain jobs – but that seems to be changing. In 2015, the world's biggest publisher, Penguin Random House, said it no longer required candidates for new jobs to have a university degree. It said it wanted to open up opprtunities to attract more varied candidates into publishing. Its HR boss added that growing evidence shows there is no simple correlation between having a degree and future professional success. The same move was also made in 2015 by private-sector giants PricewaterhouseCoopers and Ernst & Young, which are among Britain's biggest graduate recruiters.

7 Temping

If you're new to the charity or social-enterprise sector, it can be hard to persuade employers to give you a chance in a full-time position. Alternatively, you may need to start at a lower level than you're used to, and have to work your way back up.

One way to get your foot in the door is to take on temporary contracts. There's usually a range of temp opportunities available, which involve less commitment for everyone concerned, and they can be a great way to build valuable charity experience.

Marie Faulkner, who now works at Marie Curie, believes temping was an incredibly helpful step in her career journey.

'Temping allowed me to move up the ladder really quickly'

Marie Faulkner
Social Media and Online Community Manager, Marie Curie

When I started out...
Most of the opportunities seemed to be internships. I did one and got a lot of experience. But it really depends. It's great if the internship is a fixed programme, and they put real opportunities in place for you.

But if you're just someone's admin assistant, you can end up being a dogsbody. I actually think you can feel quite bad about yourself after an internship. It's not always good for your confidence.

My passion
I always knew that I had to be proud of where I worked. From the start, I wanted to be part of an ethical and moral organization. I have to be fully behind it, otherwise I lack that motivation.

My way in...
I couldn't get a permanent job in the charity sector at the start – I was recently out of university and hadn't established myself enough. So I went for a temp job and started at Action for Children. I found that people saw me as part of the furniture – I was immediately taken more seriously than an intern.

How temping helped me

My first job out of university earned me £18,000. My temp role at Action for Children was for £21,000. In my second temp role at the charity NCVO, I was offered a permanent job and moved onto £27,000. And now I'm full-time at Marie Curie I've gone up from there. I feel temping allowed me to move up the ladder really quickly. If I'd taken a full-time assistant role straight away, I'd probably have been stuck there a while.

The best thing about temping

...is that it can give you a lot of insight that you can put to good use in future job applications. You learn the kind of language that's used in the sector, how charities work – and you're getting paid at the same time.

It's also very simple to explain to future employers. When you start a temp job, you usually have a clear goal – you're either covering someone or working on a particular project. There's a set timeframe and it's a tangible thing you can explain in an interview.

Sometimes it's easier than explaining a permanent job, as you have a very clearly defined purpose.

Social-enterprise specifics

If you want to work for a social enterprise, you'll find most charity job websites (such as Third Sector and the Guardian Jobs) will automatically include social-enterprise roles too.

In addition, Social Enterprise UK, the national trade body for social enterprise, has an active jobs board just for social-enterprise positions – socialenterprise.org.uk/lists/jobs-board

If you don't just want to work for a social enterprise, but are thinking about starting one of your own, there are many ways to pick up the skills you need.

For example, the School for Social Entrepreneurs in London aims to 'empower people from all backgrounds to create positive social change'. It's an excellent way to understand how social enterprises work, get support from people who have been there and done it, and turn a brilliant idea into a dynamic ethical business. the-sse.org

'More than money' careers

You don't have to work for a charity or social enterprise to be a 'doer'. You could also follow your heart to a number of careers that are intrinsically about helping others or the environment.

Think about teachers, for example. Many of us can still recall at least one teacher who inspired and helped us at school. Teachers can earn a very good living, but it's fair to say that most teachers aren't motivated solely by money.

We have suggested some more jobs here but there's no exhaustive list, as everybody would have different ideas about what should be included.

These jobs tend to have a few things in common: they are typically in the public sector – so they're not about making shareholders rich; and they provide an essential service that helps all of us – they are not just for people who can afford it.

We won't spend too much time on these vocations. After all, if you have a strong calling to be a social worker or a doctor, for example, there's a very clearly defined route you need to take – and you don't need a book like this to tell you how.

But if you are motivated by more than money and want to do something that really makes a difference, it's good to consider all the options.

For the public good

Vocation careers include:
- Doctor
- Nurse
- Teacher
- Social worker

Let's hear from two people who have listened to their 'calling'...

'You do feel hugely valued and proud'

Chris Blewett
Paramedic

What's it really like to be a paramedic?

Everyone's preconception is that it's like *Casualty*. There definitely is a dramatic side – lots of traumatic accidents and medical emergencies. But there's also the little old lady with poor mobility who has pressed her panic-alarm button. You need life-saving skills but also people skills.

How did you get here?

I'd been working as a diver and did a rescue course – and realized I liked it, so I applied for the ambulance service. My route in was a bit different – today most new paramedics have to do a three-year degree course, with one day per week with a mentoring paramedic like me.

Why did you want to do it?

It was very much an altruistic reason. I wanted to provide good patient care and give something back to the community. You do feel hugely valued and proud – the public's response to us is fantastic.

What are the downsides?

In the last decade, the workload has trebled and the workforce shrunk. GPs don't go out to people's houses as much, and we're often used as tertiary GPs.

You're also working a lot of unsocial hours – including 12-hour shifts. You do really have to love it.

And the money?

It depends but new paramedics earn around £22-25,000, which goes up to around £32,000 nearer the top. You could earn more elsewhere, but I haven't seen it as a sacrifice because it's something I've loved doing.

What about the future?

There is some career progression in the role, but I'm currently planning a new career path, which uses my skills and experience in a different way. For 14 years, I've taken huge pride and satisfaction in being a paramedic. I've worked with a fantastic team, and can think of hundreds of people who may be alive because of my role, and that's a wonderful feeling. I only wish I'd kept a diary.

'I enjoy helping people'

Cat Cain-Williams
Social worker

Did you always want to do this?
No, I wanted to work with animals when I was younger. I did my first degree in Psychology and Zoology, as I was interested in animal behaviour, and thought about that as a career. But when I finished, none of the opportunities really gripped me.

What happened next?
I temped for a bit – and did one job cleaning at a children's home. I enjoyed interacting with the kids, and decided to see if I could get a job with Social Services. I got an interview and became an assistant care manager – similar to a social worker but not qualified.

Was the work rewarding?
Yes. I was working with unaccompanied refugee children – we took referrals from immigration at Gatwick Airport – and it was very intense, but I loved it. After a couple of years, though, I got to a point where – to progress in any way – I had to be qualified. And that's when the Council agreed to sponsor me to do my Masters degree in social work.

How has your role changed?
I went on maternity leave two years ago, and that coincided with a service redesign – which means I'm now dong more mainstream social work.

How hard is it doing social work?
It is tough. There's a lot of unfair press coverage. We definitely have too many cases, and I sometimes also feel that we're just a little cog in a wheel – that we're propping up an unjust society. With some families who've had children removed, you feel, if they'd just had a bit more help, it wouldn't have come to that. So, while I'm proud of what I do, I'm also a bit ashamed on behalf of society.

What do you get out of the work?
I enjoy helping people. When you're working with a child who is traumatized, it's very rewarding to see them open up and build trust. With refugee children, it's even more pronounced. When they have no family, and you're working with them over a long time, there's a real appreciation. I've seen some of those children go on to do degrees and really thrive.

What advice would you give?
If you want to pursue a career in social work, make sure you look after yourself. A lot of colleagues work very long hours and they're still not keeping up. There can be a lot of pressure, but it's important to have a balance!

From doers to changers

If you can only ever imagine yourself working for a non-profit or a social enterprise, this chapter may have informed and inspired you to take the next step.

In Chapter 4, though, we'll move away from this world of ethical 'doers'. We'll look at the growing number of for-profit companies who are defying 'business as usual' and making a positive difference to people and planet.

We'll discover some of the ingenious and inspiring ways that companies are now looking beyond the financial bottom line. And we'll meet some of the employees who have put ethical values at the heart of traditional businesses – and used their working lives to improve the world. These are the 'changers'.

Doer checklist

- Do you only want to work for a charity or social enterprise?
- Do you know your passions and motivators?
- Do you know which skills you'd like to use?
- Have you created a shortlist of ethical organizations?
- Do you know where to find them?
- Do you have a plan for getting charity job-ready?

4

The Changers

Engaging with the world of business

The Changers

The business world is home to an incredible range of ethical career choices.

If you know where to look, you can find thousands of businesses around the world that are committed to being 'good corporate citizens'.

From the products and services they sell, and the supply chains they use, to the way they work with their local communities or look after the environment, these companies have put principles at the top of their priorities.

They may make profits but they're proving that the private sector doesn't have to be about corporate greed. In Mahatma Gandhi's words, they have decided to 'be the change' they wish to see in the world.

So let's call them the 'changers'.

Profits with purpose

From architecture practices to digital agencies, engineering firms to accountants, these inspiring businesses work across every industry, and come in all shapes and sizes.

There's the restaurant that employs migrant and refugee women, the bank that always tops ethical industry awards, the clothing brand that wants you to repair clothes rather than buy new ones. These companies are showing the many ways you can turn ordinary businesses into extraordinary, ethically minded enterprises.

In this chapter, we'll look at some of these – and show you how to spot the ones that truly 'walk the talk' when it comes to social and environmental impact.

Hello, intrapreneurs

We'll also be looking at a powerful (and increasingly popular) new breed of ethical employee: the intrapreneur. Sometimes called 'cubicle warriors', they are transforming companies from within – adding social purpose and ethical values to ordinary for-profit businesses. They're proving that you don't need to find an *existing* ethical company to find work you love: you can help create one from the inside.

Finally, if you're thinking about working on your own, or starting your own business (either now or in the future), this chapter should also give you plenty of food for thought. Many of the people you'll meet along the way have branched out and done their own thing, either as freelancers, consultants or business owners. Every one of them has done it their way – and you can too.

Let's get started...

Business as unusual

There's no legal definition of an 'ethical company'. You won't find one global accreditation scheme or governing body. And that means they're all different.

Some businesses follow a particular passion – say, meeting an environmental goal or supporting a specific charity. But more commonly, you'll find a pick'n'mix approach to ethical business; after all, there's no limit to the ingenious and imaginative ways that companies can do good.

To help make sense of this melting pot, I've grouped ethical businesses into seven different approaches. I hope this will help you cut through any confusion – and narrow down the kind of places where you'd like to work.

1. **Earn to give**
   From donating their profits to the increasingly popular 'buy one, give one' model, these companies focus on maximizing revenue to do good.

2. **Green goals**
   These include intrinsically eco-businesses (such as renewable-energy firms), zero-carbon companies, and other environmental goals, such as biodiversity.

3. **Community matters**
   The focus here is on social impact – helping people in need. The 'community' could be anyone: from local disabled people or marginalized groups to communities in the developing world.

4. **Close to home**
   These businesses look after their own – providing the best possible workplaces to help staff flourish and feel empowered and purposeful: from personal development opportunities to deciding on ways for the business to make a positive difference.

5. **Supply-chain heroes**
   Business can make a huge difference by insisting that their ethical values go right through their supply chains – from the raw materials they use to the way suppliers' employees are treated.

6. **Sector supporters**
   Some companies exist solely to help charities and social enterprise. From

charity banking to ethical property management, they have found a niche in helping ethical organizations to flourish.

7. **Game changers**

   Some ethical businesses rip up the rulebooks by transforming the way an entire industry works. They lead the way and inspire others to follow.

1 Earn to give

Some companies feel the best way to make a difference is to make as much money as they can – and then give some of it away.

In their business biography *Ben & Jerry's Double-Dip*, ethical ice-cream pioneers Ben Cohen and Jerry Greenfield explain:

> 'We believed that business was a machine for making money. Therefore we thought the best way to make Ben & Jerry's a force for progressive social change was to grow bigger so we could make more profits and give more money away.
>
> 'We'd decided to give away 10 per cent of our profits every year. Ten per cent of the profits of a $100-million company could do a lot more than 10 per cent of the $3 or $4 million we were currently doing... [So] we decided to go to the next level.'
>
> benjerry.com

Earning to give is straightforward. You can run the business how you want, concentrate on earning as much money as possible, but instead of keeping all the profits for yourself (or dividing them among shareholders), you give them to good causes instead. That could be a partner charity, or a particular project close to your heart.

If you care about making the biggest impact possible, finding a company that gives away a percentage of its profits could be an excellent move. After all, when a vast corporation like US bank Wells Fargo commits to giving away around 1.5 per cent of its earnings every year, this can make an incredible difference to communities. In 2015, the bank gave away over $280 million to various good causes, including $25 million to a charity that helps people on low incomes to purchase affordable homes.

wellsfargo.com

Remember, though: the 'earn to give' model can be very powerful, but it may not be aligned with your own moral compass, and it can also be exploited. After all, there's nothing to stop a company director taking a huge salary, reducing the company's 'profits' to almost nothing, giving that away and saying: 'We give all of our profits to charity'.

As with any career choice, it's important to find out as much as you can about each company, and ask yourself some questions. Do they really 'walk the talk' when it comes to ethical business? Does it feel like marketing spin, or do the people running the company seem genuinely committed to making a difference?

Buy one, give one

An increasingly popular twist on this profit-donation model is the 'buy one, give one' approach – especially among consumer-facing brands. Instead of giving away a percentage of profits, this is where the company will match your purchase with a donation to a good cause.

The shoe company TOMS is a good example of this – as it promises, 'With every pair you purchase, TOMS will give a pair of new shoes to a child in need.'

Through its 'One-for-One' programme, the company has so far given more than 60 million pairs of new shoes to children in need. Using a network of partners in over 70 countries, the business has also developed a wide-ranging corporate social responsibility programme, which spans a range of other issues, including improving maternal health and access to water. **toms.com**

The right to see

Many companies make and sell glasses. But US business Warby Parker is another business that's a little different – thanks to its founding belief that 'everyone has the right to see'.

From its start in 2010, the company has partnered with health charities around the globe.

'Almost one billion people worldwide lack access to glasses, which means that 15 per cent of the world's population cannot effectively learn or work,' explains Warby Parker. 'To help address this problem, [we] work with non-profits to ensure that for every pair of glasses sold, a pair is distributed to someone in need.' Today, Warby Parker has distributed more than two million pairs of glasses worldwide.

Interestingly, instead of using the 'buy one, give one' model, the company doesn't give the glasses away; it sells them at 'affordable prices'.

'It's a sticky fact of life that kind-hearted gestures can have unintended consequences,' explains Warby Parker. 'Donating is often a temporary solution, not a lasting one. It can contribute to a culture of dependency [and] it is rarely sustainable.

'Instead of donating, our non-profit partners train men and women to sell glasses for ultra-affordable prices, which allows them to earn a living. More important, it forces our partners to offer glasses that people actually want to buy.'

warbyparker.com

This is an important point. Donated goods are often a questionable form of helping and they can have unintended consequences, such as potentially harming local economies, taking away decision-making from local people, or giving unsuitable goods. Many businesses have recognized that a better, more sustainable alternative is to create jobs, empower people and help to support local economies to grow.

Other companies that 'earn to give'

- A pioneer in ethical tourism, **Responsible Travel** is committed to 'increasing the benefits of tourism to local people and places'. As well as running its entire business along ethical principles, between 2006 and 2015 it donated 13 per cent of profits to charity.   responsibletravel.com

- **Green Kite** is a London-based inventory company that performs property inspections for estate agents and landlords. It donates five per cent of its profits to Centrepoint, a charity that supports homeless young people with housing, learning, health and life skills.   green-kite.co.uk

- **People Water** aims to marry profits with purpose ('We're a for-profit, cause-based business, committed to alleviating the global water crisis.') For every bottle purchased, the company gives an equal amount of clean water to a person in need – either by drilling a new well, repairing an existing one, or installing a water purification system.   peoplewater.com

- Mobile phone network **The People's Operator** is founded on the idea that 'mobile could be used to change lives for the better'. The company directs 10 per cent of every customer's bill to the good cause of their choice – at no additional cost.   thepeoplesoperator.com

2 Green goals

If you want to work for a company that cares for the environment, there are many different kinds of approach to choose from.

Some businesses focus on supporting a particular cause – for example, animal conservation or reforestation. Others have a specific target in mind, such as becoming a 'carbon zero' company – becoming more energy efficient, using clean energy, eliminating any waste going to landfill, and offsetting remaining emissions.

A company's eco-credentials could also extend to its core business activities – such as inventing sustainable technology, generating renewable energy or using biodegradable products.

Outdoor clothing company **Finisterre** is a strong example. The Cornwall-based brand has integrated sustainability throughout its business. From turning waste plastics into swimwear and repairing customers' old jackets, to developing an 'i-Spy' traceability programme to ensure ethical fabric sourcing, it is deeply committed to ecologically sustainable fashion.

One of Finisterre's most interesting and unusual initiatives is its Bowmont jumper, made of 100-per-cent British merino wool. When the company decided to make it, there was no supply chain of fine-fibre wool in the UK.

After two years of detective-like research, Finisterre discovered farmer Lesley Prior, the guardian of the last 28 Bowmont Merino sheep in the world. Eight years on, her flock is close to 250-strong, and the business has realized its dream of creating locally sourced, superfine merino wool clothing.   finisterre.com

Other companies with green goals

- **Wyke Farms**: The dairy business – and award-winning Cheddar cheese maker – in Somerset has saved £100,000 a year on energy bills thanks to a list of green initiatives, including generating energy from solar power and cow dung (biogas), and a water recycling plant.   wykefarms.com

- **Winnow**: A business specifically designed to solve an environmental problem, Winnow's aim is to 'help the hospitality industry tackle avoidable food waste'. To date, it has reportedly helped its customers save £2 million through its

innovative automated monitoring tool that enables chefs to minimize food
waste. winnowsolutions.com

- **Interface**: This is a global carpet-tile company that has committed to having 'no negative impact' on the planet by the year 2020. Its 'Mission Zero' promise has seen the business reduce its water intake by 87 per cent, cut its carpets' average carbon footprint in half, and reduce 92 per cent of greenhouse-gas emissions from its manufacturing sites, among many other initiatives.
interface.com

- **Green Accountancy**: Blazing a trail for ethically minded accountants everywhere, this firm helps its clients reduce their environmental impacts by providing persuasive business cases for caring about the planet. One of its initiatives is a dedicated 'Carbon Accounting' system for small businesses.
greenaccountancy.com

3 Community matters

Some companies are focused primarily on making a difference to other people's lives. From supporting an economically disadvantaged community to proactively employing people with disabilities, there are hundreds of different ways to make a real impact on society.

The **University of Manchester** may not seem like a regular business, but it's actually the city's biggest employer. In 2012, the university started an employ- ment centre in the heart of Moss Side, one of Manchester's most troubled areas.

Called The Works, it helps local people find job opportunities at the university and beyond. Unemployed people can receive advice, get onto training courses, and learn about the 600-700 catering, administration and construction job openings the university has every year. To date, it has helped around 2,400 people find a job, the vast majority of whom (97 per cent) were previously unemployed. manchester.ac.uk

The idea – and location – of a 'community' depends on the business. **Divine**, for example, is the only mainstream chocolate company 44-per-cent owned by the farmers who supply its cocoa. Although its shoppers are predominantly in the UK and US, its community are the 80,000 members of the Ghanaian farmers' co- operative, Kuapa Kokoo; and a commitment to supporting these people is at the heart of the business.

Each year, Divine passes 44 per cent of its distributed profit to the Kuapa Kokoo's 80,000 members – just one of the co-operative's four income streams. In addition, they are paid the Fairtrade minimum of $2,000 per tonne for their cocoa, a $200 Fairtrade premium per tonne, plus two per cent of the company's annual turnover for development. divinechocolate.com

Closer to home, one social business has identified a different kind of community that needs help. It's not in the developing world, or focused on global poverty. But it's still a hugely important issue.

Back in 2005, Emma Stewart and Karen Mattison, colleagues and mothers, had a Eureka moment. Just like them, their friends had left work to look after their children, and – like them – they were finding it tough getting back to work in a role that suited both their professional skills and their new family life.

They decided to start a different kind of recruitment agency, called Women Like Us, to support mums going back to work. Designed to help women find part-time job opportunities, the London-based agency helps mothers to regain their confidence, and sell their skills to employers. As well as placing women into suitable roles, it offers free online courses, career-support workshops and face-to-face support to women on very low incomes. (You can hear what it's like to work at Women Like Us on Page 51.) womenlikeus.org.uk

Other companies that value their communities

- Akin to an ethical *Dragons' Den*, **Clearly Social** is the UK's first angel investor network focused on creating social and environmental impact, alongside financial return. Its investors support inspiring ethically minded entrepreneurs to get their innovative solutions to social and environmental problems to market. clearlysocialangels.com

- **intu** operates 15 shopping centres around the UK, including in Norwich where it has started a pioneering work-experience programme for serving prisoners.

  A partnership with HMP Norwich, the intu Chapelfield Custody & Community Project provides up to eight weeks of work experience and training opportunities for serving prisoners from two local prisons. They gain skills and experience in a range of jobs, including maintenance, customer service, recycling, and painting and decorating. This helps break the cycle of crime by helping offenders secure permanent jobs while on licence, which benefits the whole community. Only five per cent of intu Chapelfield work experience prisoners have reoffended, compared to national statistics of 47 per cent.

intu.co.uk

• The people whose lives North London restaurant **Mazi Mas** wants to change are migrant and refugee women. Current staff include female chefs from Iran, Ethiopia, Turkey, Senegal, Peru, Nicaragua, Turkey, Brazil and Nepal, many of whom were recruited from migrant and refugee outreach programmes in London.

Founder Nikandre Kopcke is a sociology and gender studies graduate who decided 'it was time for me to stop talking feminism, and start doing it'.

Today Mazi Mas provides opportunities for women who aspire to careers in the food industry to gain paid work experience, develop their skills and tell their stories. 'The transition from long-term unemployment to full-time employment is a very difficult one, especially for migrant and refugee women,' says Kopcke. 'Our model combines paid work experience, employment support and access to professional networks, skills training, and a supportive social network. This builds women's confidence, enhances their employability, increases access to job opportunities, and improves their wellbeing.'

mazimas.co.uk

• Ethical jewellery brand **Made** could make its products more cheaply, but it has decided to invest in its workforce in Kenya. As well as providing safe working environments, long-term job security and training for its growing team, the company buys raw materials from local people at a fair price – strengthening the local economy and empowering small businesses. You can read more about the Made story from Neal Gershinson on the next page.   made.uk.com

Neal's path

Neal Gershinson, managing director of ethical-jewellery brand Made, reflects on his career choices.

I've worked in the fashion business since I was 16.

My career started properly at Burberry's around 1990. Ten years later, I started my own handbag business.

I started to become cynical about the supply chain.

I wasn't enjoying going out to manufacturers in China – working with faceless organizations and lining the pockets of wealthy individuals. I'd had enough of walking around soulless factories where the workers looked like robots.

I heard about the company Made

I met the founder, and this is mostly her story. As a tourist she would go to Nairobi in Kenya, and see artisans and craftspeople casting and manufacturing jewellery. But it was all carved lions and tourist trinkets – not right for the UK fashion market. So she began encouraging them to make more contemporary jewellery. That was mostly in Kibera, the largest slum in east Africa.

The company wasn't working

The founder was struggling to run the business, and I got involved that same day. Over the years, I took more control, and I now fully own the business. To supply retailers in a reliable way, I knew

the only way was to set up a workshop in Kenya.

We look after our people...

We now have around 80 staff in Africa. Their contracts are equal to our staff in the UK in terms of protection and support, and medical cover – which we've also extended to immediate family. There's training support, and we have started doing interest-free loans. When you go there, you see how many problems people have in their lives, but everyone is smiling and giving high fives. It's inspiring. I come back fully charged – raring to go to improve the business.

Collaborations need to be right

Some brands will approach us because we suit them at that moment, they want to dip in and out. But we need sustainable partnerships. Morally, I've got to be committed to staff levels – so I need to assess potential new customers and see if they want to create a real partnership. I don't want to create an atmosphere of fear and insecurity in the workshop.

With my cynical hat on...

Some major retailers use us to do a bit of greenwashing, but it can suit us as well. We're not holier than thou, and we're not in a position to preach. I also don't think that our approach is the most important thing about Made – I talk about being affordable, efficient and good quality. Our approach shouldn't be something to sing and dance about, it should be standard.

My advice for ethical entrepreneurs

Start small and try to keep it as tight as you can in the early days, and let it grow sustainably. You don't have to have a big business immediately: things should grow organically.

It also doesn't matter what you do as long as you're committed internally. Ethical production is about doing the right thing. When we started out, I wanted to encourage existing factories to go down an ethical route, but that was too challenging. So we set out on our own journey.

There's nothing wrong with being selfish

I get a feel-good factor about my job. When I go home at night, I'm proud to tell my children what I do. I like them to see the impact their dad's having on a lot of people. And it works both ways. If there are days when the orders are down or sales aren't brilliant, I can still look at the positive impact of our business – and that's a huge motivation.

4 Close to home

Your idea of an ethical employer may not just revolve around how they treat others. The way that businesses look after their own staff often says just as much about their morals and values. Giving staff a healthy work-life balance, investing in their career development through training, and enabling them to take on socially and environmentally motivated projects at work are just some of the ways that companies can make a difference.

Work to live, or live to work?

Staff perks are standard fare at many successful companies, especially in the digital industry. Besides the almost obligatory table-tennis tables and comfy 'break-out' spaces, you can often expect free lunches, drinks on a Friday, and other treats. These can be good for bonding with colleagues, but they also often act as gilded handcuffs – tying staff to the office for longer. After all, the more hours you're at work, the more work you can do for the company.

One software business that's bucking this trend is **Basecamp**. Its US-based CEO Jason Fried actively encourages its employees *not* to work too much. He wants people to take more time off, expand their horizons and spend their time at work feeling fresh and inspired.

Here are some of the standard benefits for Basecamp employees:

- Four-day, 30-hour work weeks in the summer.
- $100 a month for fitness, which employees can spend on gym memberships, yoga classes, etc.
- $100 a month for massages.
- CSA (community supported agriculture) memberships, so workers get locally grown fruits and vegetables.
- The option to work at any of the company's offices around the world.
- A one-month sabbatical every three years.
- Basecamp also pays for their employees' holidays as a gift.

This may all sound too good to be true, but Basecamp aren't insisting on these staff benefits out of charity. Fried believes that his employees will be happier, more productive, and more loyal if the business treats them well – and the model is working.

This tweet from the Basecamp CEO sums it up neatly:

> **Jason Fried** ✔
> @jasonfried
>
> 🐦 Follow
>
> Working more than 40 hours a week doesn't mean you're working hard. It just means you are working more than 40 hours a week.
>
> 1:22 PM - 12 Jan 2016   ↩   ⇄ 752   ♥ 717

It may still be the exception rather than the rule, but the Basecamp story shows that commercial (in this case privately owned) businesses can have strong moral values that shape how people are treated at work.   basecamp.com

Here in the UK, Brighton-based digital marketing agency **Propellernet** is treading a similar path. Frequently voted in the top 10 places to work in the UK by the Great Place to Work Institute (**greatplacetowork.co.uk**), the company has a vision for creating work that staff love.

'Our whole ethos, our whole reason for being, is enjoying the workplace,' says CEO Nikki Gatenby. 'We fundamentally believe that if you help people achieve their dreams, you will definitely win their hearts and minds.'

Propellernet takes 'dreams' very seriously. That's why it has a Dream Ball machine – an old-fashioned sweet dispenser – filled with 300 handwritten dreams from employees. Every year, the business makes some of those dreams come true. This motivation scheme also ties in with the company's focus on health and wellbeing: Propellernet puts five per cent of its profits every month into a wellbeing fund, which employees spend as they see fit. This includes nutritionists, health checks, yoga, pilates and reflexology in the office.

'Lots of agencies are only about pursuing cold hard cash,' says Nikki. 'But we believe that if you put people and purpose first, good things will come.'

To read more of Nikki's story, see Page 168.   propellernet.co.uk

Other companies that look after those close to home

- IT company **Softcat** employs over 800 people, is listed on the London Stock Exchange, and has also been voted the 'UK's Best Workplace 2016' by the Great Place to Work Institute. The company rewards its staff with incentive trips and uncapped commission for sales teams, gives world-class training, promotes social responsibility – encouraging employees to support good causes through fundraising – and aims to break down hierarchies, with managers and directors sitting with teams 100 per cent of the time.

softcat.com

- Bolton-based baby pushchair brand **Cosatto** is committed to delivering a 'revolutionary work/life balance' and 'a values system based on respect and understanding' for its 51 staff. Some of its more unusual features include an office slide from one floor to another, granting one staff member a 'once in a lifetime' dream every year – voted for by the whole company – and giving money to a different employee's charity of choice every month.

cosatto.com

- Healthcare consultants **Axon** have offices in Europe and North America, and frequently scoop 'best place to work' awards. From outstanding training and mentoring programmes and employee recognition, to giving staff *pro bono* time to support local charities, the business has grown successfully without compromising on its values. axon-com.com

"The world doesn't
need new businesses
as much as it needs
new ways of doing
business.

Lara Galinsky

5 Supply-chain heroes

Any company that wants to make a positive difference in the world needs to think about its supply chain. That means understanding the impact of all the people, organizations, activities and resources that go into getting goods or services to the final customer.

In recent years, there have been many supply-chain scandals – with well-known brands shown to be using (knowingly or not) suppliers that run sweatshops, use child labour or pollute the environment.

From source to store, ethical companies take the trouble to check every link in their supply chain. And that can take a lot of work.

The ethical fashion brand **People Tree** is a good example. A pioneer of the 'slow fashion' movement, the company stands against exploitation and environmental pollution – which, it says, underpin the 'fast fashion' industry.

The brand also cuts through any 'eco-fashion' spin. As founder Safia Minney explains: 'While many fashion brands talk about "corporate social responsibility", we go further. We follow the principles of fair trade in every aspect of our business.'

As well as being the world's first clothing company to receive the World Fair Trade Organization's Fair Trade product mark in 2013, People Tree developed the first integrated supply chain for organic cotton from farm to final product. They were the first organization anywhere to achieve GOTS (Global Organic Textile Standard) certification on a supply chain entirely in the developing world.

peopletree.co.uk

If you want to work for an ethical company, check out their supply-chain credentials. If they've taken the trouble to verify and improve the way that everyone operates, right back to the source, they are likely to be shouting about it.

As you'd expect, the companies that can make the biggest social and environmental impact through their supply chains are transnationals – who often employ a complex, global web of suppliers and armies of contractors and subcontractors.

The retailer **Marks and Spencer** (M&S) calls its ethical and environmental programme 'Plan A'. Improving its food supply chain is just one part of that plan – but it's already paying dividends. As part of its goal to become the 'world's most sustainable major retailer', M&S has developed a Gold, Silver and Bronze factory standard for its food suppliers.

It pledges that, by 2020, all products will come from Silver or Gold factories. The awards are given based on ethical, economic and environmental scores, including water, waste and labour standards. As a result of this ethical squeeze on its supply chain, M&S is reporting some impressive results. For example, 60 per cent of its supplier food sites now send no waste to landfill and have cut waste by almost a third. Over half of M&S food suppliers have reduced both their water and energy usage, and employee surveys show that supplier employees are also happier than ever.   marksandspencr.com

Some companies tackle their supply-chain challenges in rather unusual ways. The transnational drinks manufacturer **SAB Miller**, for example, has won praise for an innovative project in Uganda. Its product Eagle Lager – a cross between locally made sorghum beer and conventional lager – is the result of a programme to replace expensive imported raw materials with locally sourced ingredients.

SAB Miller said it had wanted to demonstrate it could establish a completely new supply chain that used local farmers. The new beer is commercially successful (both inside and outside Uganda), supports large numbers of smallholder farmers and their communities, and sees profits put back into HIV/AIDS testing, clean water and education programmes.   sabmiller.com

Other companies that have transformed their supply chains

- Property developer **British Land** develops buildings in partnership with hundreds of external suppliers, such as architects, engineers and trade contractors. Working at such a huge scale, the company is in a powerful position to improve the industry by insisting on certain sustainability credentials. Its targets include diverting 98 per cent of demolition waste from landfill, all timber coming from certified sustainable sources, and new office buildings achieving BREEAM Excellent ratings. In three years, British Land has reduced development waste sent to landfill from 15 per cent to 2 per cent – equivalent to the weight of over 26,000 double-decker buses.

  britishland.com

- You don't have to be big to care about your supply chain. UK small business **Green Oil** was the world's first company to make fully biodegradable, fully plant-based bicycle chain oil – and it now produces a range of green bike maintenance products from its factory in Wales. Founder Simon Nash is committed to cleaning the supply chain involved in bike products, and has clocked up a number of firsts – his was the first bike company in the UK to use 100-per-cent recycled plastic for its bottles, and its 'Bicycle Brush' is the world's first bicycle product with FSC (Forest Stewardship Council) certification. The company has also made the first fairly traded bicycle product – the EcoSponge – made from recycled fabric and plant-based sponge.

  green-oil.net

- Whatever your views on Scandinavian furniture giant **IKEA**, it has taken a number of giant steps to improve its supply chain. One example is cotton: IKEA uses an incredible amount of cotton in its products – estimated at around 0.7 per cent of the world's cotton supply. Conventional cotton farming uses a large amount of chemicals and water, and has major environmental and social consequences. In 2005, IKEA teamed up with the World Wide Fund for Nature (WWF) and other organizations to form the 'Better Cotton Initiative'.

  Since then the retailer has invested over €1.34 million (£970,000) in sustainable cotton farming projects and helped around 110,000 cotton farmers adopt more sustainable practices. Today, all the cotton used for IKEA products comes from more sustainable sources, making it the first major retailer to reach this milestone – and helping transform the global cotton industry.

  ikea.com

6 Sector supporters

Some companies' sole purpose is to help other organizations do good in the world. They are regular for-profit businesses, but they exist to support charities, social enterprises and NGOs in alleviating social and environmental problems.

These 'sector supporters' span a wide range of industries, as charitable organizations need a very broad span of products and services. From providing office space and setting up IT systems to providing legal services, they are committed – either solely or partly – to helping good causes.

If you want to make a difference – but don't need to be right on the front line – this kind of business could be the perfect match.

The London-based company **Environment Films** is a good example. Started by filmmaker Ella Todd, they were concerned that many charities and NGOs couldn't afford to create high-quality video – which meant their campaigns were failing to reach audiences.

To counter this, Environment Films provides a non-profit service to charities and NGOs. To afford this, the company, in its own words, blends 'pragmatism with purpose' – taking on paid work for selected corporate clients in order to support its *pro bono* charity work.

Here, it has a clear policy on the kinds of businesses it won't work for, including: any company that is directly involved or promotes industry associated with fossil fuels, arms and weapons, alcohol and tobacco, as well as companies that use animals in entertainment, food, clothing, cosmetics or household products.

environmentfilms.org

There is a sliding scale for sector supporters. Some have built their entire businesses around supporting a cause. Others are more balanced – putting ethical values at their core but not working exclusively for charities and non-profits.

The law firm **Bates Wells Braithwaite** (BWB) is one such company. Its team works across multiple industries – from media to healthcare – but it is renowned as a world leader in social enterprise. Indeed, BWB actually devised and later helped the government to implement a new form of social enterprise, the Community Interest Company, or CIC (see Page 50). As well having social good at its heart, BWB is unlike many other law firms in that it also provides free legal advice to some charities, social enterprises and individuals. bwbllp.com

Other companies that support the charity sector

- The **Ethical Property Company** (EPC) is one of the largest social businesses in the UK. It owns and/or manages 24 centres across the UK, providing office, meeting, event and retail space to over 1,000 organizations each year. It's a money-making business (ECP made a profit of over £750,000 in 2015) but it's firmly aligned to the third sector. From well-known campaign groups, like Amnesty International, to smaller enterprises such as marine biodiversity organization Blue Ventures (not to mention the publisher of this book, New Internationalist), it provides high-quality and affordable premises to a wealth of charities and social enterprises.

  As part of its wider business family, EPC also includes the offshoot Ethical IT. This partnership supports voluntary organizations in a different way – by providing cost-effective and sustainable IT and telephone services to help them stay connected. ethicalproperty.co.uk
  ethicalit.net

- **Aimia** is one of the world's most successful creators of loyalty programmes – employing over 4,000 employees in 20 countries. Although the data insight company operates across many corporate sectors, one of its most interesting projects involved supporting the homelessness charity, Centrepoint.

  The charity wanted to see if its data held any clues about helping improve services for homeless young people – and Aimia's analysts set to work. The insights from this pioneering 'data philanthropy' project identified a host of improvements and generated £1.5 million of new funding for Centrepoint in 2014.

  Over the past two years, Aimia's team has supported over 50 charities and donated more than 15,000 hours of *pro bono* analytic support – filling a valuable skills gap in the sector, and adding a financial value estimated in excess of £30 million. aimia.com

"To succeed, you have to believe in something with such a passion that it becomes a reality.

Anita Roddick

7 Game changers

Some companies simply rip up the rulebooks. They succeed in bringing ethical values into an industry so emphatically – often in the face of adversity – that other businesses follow and copy them. This can change a whole industry, creating a bigger positive social and environmental impact than they could ever have imagined in their start-up days.

Even if these companies weren't always the *first* to attempt this more purposeful approach in their sectors, they were the ones who succeeded at scale. They are the game changers. Let's meet a few.

A hand up, not a hand out

How do you change a 300-year-old industry overnight? That's what happened in 1991 when John Bird and Gordon Roddick launched **The Big Issue**.

Instead of creating just another publishing company, and printing just another magazine, they decided to use their business to transform people's lives. By enabling homeless people to become magazine sellers, they gave them 'a hand up, not a hand out'.

Today, over 2,000 people sell *The Big Issue* in the UK. It's a business unlike any other, and has inspired the creation of over 120 'street papers' in other countries – helping tens of thousands of people to move away from life on the streets.

bigissue.org.uk

The Big Issue may strictly count itself as a social enterprise – but there are many examples of purely for-profit businesses that have transformed industries through ethics. And *The Big Issue*'s Gordon Roddick was married to a woman who did just that.

Anita Roddick opened the first **Body Shop** in 1976. The human-rights activist and environmental campaigner wanted to create and sell ethically sourced beauty products that met her five core values:

- Against animal testing
- Support community trade
- Activate self-esteem
- Defend human rights
- Protect the planet

Anita started with a small shop in Brighton. Fast-forward three decades, and the Body Shop had almost 2,000 stores, and was serving over 77 million customers throughout the world. It was voted the second most trusted brand in the UK.

In 2006, the cosmetics giant L'Oréal bought the Body Shop for £652 million. For some, this was a disappointment, even a 'sell-out' – L'Oréal has been involved in animal testing and is part-owned by Nestlé, which has been heavily criticized over its corporate behaviour, especially over its marketing of babyfoods in the developing world. However, Anita argued that the Body Shop would be a 'Trojan horse' – sticking to its original values and influencing the way that L'Oréal does business across all its brands.

Whatever the controversy around the sale, no one can deny that The Body Shop put animal rights and environmental protection at the heart of the cosmetics world, and changed the industry forever.

Today, The Body Shop employs thousands of staff around the globe – and is still committed to Anita Roddick's original five values.   thebodyshop.com

The story of smoothies giant **Innocent Drinks** has a similar conclusion. Today, Innocent is over 90-per-cent owned by The Coca-Cola Company, not too many people's shining example of an ethical business.

Depending on your moral compass, this may make Innocent seem rather less, well, innocent, by association. But, taken alone, the Innocent brand is still run along many of the same ethical principles it started out with – and which helped transform an industry.

Since starting out in 1999, Innocent has aimed to 'to leave things a little bit better than we find them'.

The company's three founders extended that principle across all areas of the business: for example, Innocent has always donated a minimum of 10 per cent of its profits each year to charity. Today, most of that goes to the Innocent Foundation, which it set up in 2004 to help build 'sustainable futures for the world's poorest people'. (To date, the foundation has given almost £3 million, reached over half a million people, and partnered with 41 charities across 30 countries.)

Profit-share is just part of Innocent's 'purpose'. It also takes ethical sourcing seriously – buying fruit from suppliers who look after both their workers and the environment. To help other brands follow suit, it has also teamed up with the Sustainable Agriculture Initiative and their 50 member companies to create and pilot a common standard for sustainable farming systems that everyone can use.

Innocent has also pioneered the use of recycled packaging in drinks bottles. All of its cartons are made from Forest Stewardship Council certified material, and it closely monitors its packaging suppliers' energy, water and waste.

Closer to home, Innocent is well known for looking after its staff – from the 'serious stuff' (such as private healthcare and career development programmes) to more informal perks, such as free restaurant trips for 'services to fruit' and £1,000 Innocent scholarships for staff to pursue their dreams. The company's HQ 'Fruit Towers' is also run using green electricity. Today, Innocent employs over 350 people across Europe, and regularly scoops Great Place to Work awards.

innocentdrinks.co.uk

Interestingly, the Innocent and The Body Shop stories seem to show that global corporations will take ethical businesses seriously – if they can prove their success. Today, you'll find several examples of socially and environmentally aware businesses that have been bought (or part-bought) by 'big business'. These include the fair-trade chocolate pioneers **Green & Black's** (bought by confectionery giants Cadbury's and then Kraft), ethical ice-cream pioneers **Ben & Jerry's** (now owned by Unilever) and organic food brand **Seeds of Change** (owned by Mars).

greenandblacks.co.uk

seedsofchange.co.uk

Trip to Patagonia

One game changer that hasn't been bought by a transnational is the outdoor clothing brand **Patagonia**. Founder Yvon Chouinard talks eloquently and honestly about his quest to create an environmentally and socially responsible business. And as I can't put his story into any better words, here's his explanation:

'We went organic in 1996. [But] once you start, you can't stop....

'From cotton, we moved to what happens in Patagonia's name in every step of the supply chain, from crop to fabric to finished garment. We measured the environmental impacts of selected articles of clothing and published them. We worked with an outside auditor and an in-house corporate responsibility specialist to establish the working conditions and pay for every person who sews a Patagonia garment. We learned how to make fleece jackets from recycled plastic bottles. We examined our use of paper in catalogues, the sources of our electricity, the amount of oil we consumed driving to work.

'We continued to support employees with medical insurance, maternity and paternity leave, subsidized childcare and paid internships with non-profit environmental groups. As we have for many years, we gave one per cent of sales to grassroots activists. This one-per-cent commitment isn't typical philanthropy. Rather, it's part of the cost of doing business, part of our effort to balance (however imperfectly) the impact we have on natural systems – and to protect the world on which our business, employees and customers rely.

'After many years of giving money to activists, we realized that if we could share profits, we could also supply time and muscle.

'Underlying much of what challenges Patagonia is the modern commitment to growth and consumption. We've begun to look seriously at these twin conundrums and took out an ad on Black Friday in 2011 that read, 'Don't Buy This Jacket'.

'In the end, Patagonia may never be completely responsible. We have a long way to go and we don't have a map – but we do have a way to read the terrain and to take the next step, and then the next.'

This passion, purpose and attention to detail is definitely not business as usual. But Patagonia has stuck to its values and grown to become a highly successful business. Today, it has a turnover in excess of $600 million and employs 2,000 people across the world. It has shown a different way for brands to operate in the world without compromising on their social and environmental responsibilities.

patagonia.com

Other 'game-changing' ethical companies

- In the late 1990s, two companies came along that revolutionized the UK energy market – with two very different approaches. **Good Energy**'s promise was 100-per-cent renewable energy all the time. **Ecotricity** focused more on building new sources of renewable energy in the UK. Thanks to this investment and innovation, Ecotricity now claims to deliver the 'greenest energy in Britain'. Both companies pride themselves on their ethics, their fair pricing and the way they treat their staff. And they have transformed the energy market for good.

  goodenergy.co.uk
  ecotricity.co.uk

- Founded by tricologist Mark Constantine and beauty therapist Liz Weir in the mid-1990s, **Lush** began life as a cosmetics shop and spa in Poole, Dorset.

  Today they have stores across the globe and are one of the best-known ethical beauty brands. They describe their own scheme 'Fighting Animal Testing' as 'not just a Lush position and policy, but a lifetime goal and the core value of our company'.

As well as never buying ingredients from companies that test on animals, Lush has committed to eradicating animal testing through education, lobbying and supporting campaign groups that oppose animal testing.

Other policies include ethical sourcing of ingredients, support for charity projects through its 'Charity Pots' initiative, and stringent environmental commitments to recycling, saving energy, and reducing carbon emissions from transporting goods.   uk.lush.com

- Engineering firm **ARUP**'s roots go all the way back to the 1940s. Its name has always been synonymous with quality, but it hasn't always been known for its commitment to helping the environment and communities in need.

  In the early 2000s it adopted the strapline 'We shape a better world' but it wasn't until 2009 that its philanthropic and sustainability activities really took shape – with the formation of its International Development arm. Jo Da Silva, former senior co-ordinator at the UN Refugee Agency and lecturer in sustainable development, was the mastermind behind this new not-for-profit part of the organization.

  Under her leadership, ARUP has worked in partnership with The Rockefeller Foundation and Habitat For Humanity to assist in reconstruction after natural disasters in the world's poorest countries, and to help local communities become more resilient to climate change.   arup.com

I hope these companies have inspired you – and convinced you that for-profit businesses *can* change the world for good.

These trailblazers – and a growing number of companies that have followed their lead – are out there right now, recruiting and developing the staff who will write the next chapter in their story. Do you want to be among them?

If the answer is yes, then you just need to find them. And that's what the next section of this chapter is all about.

"Anyone can look at their job and find ways to integrate sustainability thinking. It might be easier to create social change if you have a title, but anyone in an organization can have an impact.

Kirsten Olsen Cahill

Finding the good guys

Where are all the businesses that are guided by strong ethical principles, look after their staff, and aim to have a positive social and environmental impact on the world?

This section is a practical resource for finding the kind of company that matches your moral outlook, and could help you find a career you love.

Whether you're interested in computer programming or campaigning, engineering or education, this is where you'll be able to find the good guys.

Let's get started…

Ethical kitemarks

Just as you can tell a lot about a product if it's certified 'fair trade', so businesses can also apply for a variety of kitemark schemes to prove their ethical credentials.

Some of these kitemarks raise the bar higher than others. Some may focus on a specific aspect of ethical business, such as environmental performance, and may not consider the whole company. But as long as you know what matters to you, these should be a good shortcut to the companies that share your values. Typically, you'll find kitemarks awarded for many of the things we've talked about already, such as environmental track record, transparency, supply chain and so on.

The following list isn't exhaustive, but it covers a lot of kitemarks – and should save you some time and effort in identifying a shortlist of potential ethical employers:

- **B Corp** This is a global, non-profit organization that accredits and lists for-profit companies that meet high standards of social and environmental performance, accountability, and transparency. (B Corp says it is 'to business what Fairtrade certification is to coffee'.) bcorporation.uk

- **Best Workplaces Programme** Finding a job you love often involves choosing a company that is known for treating its staff well. Great Place To Work runs a programme and rankings system for businesses of all sizes that want to be assessed and gain recognition for their staff's satisfaction.

  greatplacetowork.co.uk

- **The British Standards Institute (BSI)** produces globally recognized accreditation across a wide range of industries. Products and practices are tested and BSI Kitemarks can be awarded for environmental management, occupational management and anti-bribery, among others. BSI doesn't clearly list these companies, but it's something to look out for on a potential employer's website.   bsigroup.com/en-GB/standards/#standards

- **The Fair Tax Mark** scheme highlights UK companies that it rates as 'good' taxpayers and proud of paying their fair share of tax. The issue of large businesses legally avoiding corporation tax (Facebook paid just £4,327 in UK corporation tax in 2014) is rarely out of the news.   fairtaxmark.net

- **The Ethical Company Organisation** uses a cross-spectrum of criteria – including people, animals and environment – to audit and accredit UK companies. It also produces *The Good Shopping Guide*, which aims to highlight the most ethical products and services for consumers.
  ethical-company-organisation.org/accreditation

- **Fairtrade Foundation** If you want to work in the food industry, it's worth looking out for companies that have signed up to the globally recognized Fairtrade accreditation. The Fairtrade movement pledges better prices and conditions for farmers in the developing world. Not everyone agrees with its approach, but Fairtrade has changed thousands of lives across the world.
  fairtrade.org.uk

- **Green Mark** Similar to the British Standards Institute but specifically for environmental management, Green Mark looks to provide accreditation on two levels. Green Mark Level 1 is awarded to companies who are improving their environmental performance. Green Mark Level 2 is given to companies that develop and implement an Environmental Management System (EMS).
  greenmark.co.uk

- **The AA1000** is awarded by ethical think tank AccountAbility to organizations that can prove a commitment to sustainable development and corporate responsibility. It features a range of frameworks and methodology for companies looking to create more sustainable, responsible and accountable business practices.   accountability.org

- **The Community Mark** – run by the charity Business in the Community – publicly recognizes companies that have made significant investment in communities, transforming the areas in which they operate, and creating positive impacts for society.

  bitc.org.uk/services/awards-recognition/communitymark

- **Investors in People (IIP)** This is a globally recognized mark to promote good practices in people management. According to IIP, it is the sign of 'a great employer, an outperforming place to work and a clear commitment to sustainability'.

  investorsinpeople.com

- **Ethiscore** This fascinating tool enables you to compare the corporate social responsibility records of over 25,000 companies. Run by Corporate Critic (and part of Ethical Consumer's research arm), it provides daily updated scores based on a company or product's performance.

  corporatecritic.org

- **Bright Ethics Company** Specifically designed for small businesses, this outfit provides a certification for companies that meet standards in environmental sustainability, community involvement, sourcing policies and staffing.

  brightethics.com

- **Investing in Integrity** The Institute of Business Ethics and Chartered Institute of Securities and Investment have combined to create the Investing in Integrity charter mark. Their self-assessment test helps organizations to successfully embed an ethical programme throughout the business.

  ibe.org.uk/accreditation/51

- **SEE What You Are Buying Into** This is a transparent labelling scheme for businesses that are willing to share their social, environmental and ethical (SEE) practices and policies. Once a company fills out a questionnaire, the results are posted to a website for the public to scrutinize, monitor and comment on.

  seewhatyouarebuyinginto.com

- **The Ethics Mark** The Ethics Foundation supplies this mark to organizations that have passed its screening procedure, and have been voted on by The Ethics Foundation Trustees.

  ethicsfoundation.com/the-mark/accreditation

- **The Green Achiever** This scheme offers environmental accreditation to UK businesses looking to boost their green credentials and reduce their environmental impact.   greenachiever.co.uk

- **My Green Directory** This is a listings site for companies that pursue clear environmental targets, have an ethical ethos and want to run their business for people and planet alongside profit.   mygreendirectory.info

- **YourEthicalMoney.org** A non-profit initiative of the EIRIS Foundation, this aims to provide objective, independent information on green and ethical finance to mainstream consumers. If you're interested in companies within the financial sector, it is a very helpful resource.   YourEthicalMoney.org

- **Soil Association** This charity is dedicated to highlighting organic farming. Its 'Organic Certified' logos show that standards of production for food in farming, catering and products such as textiles and health and beauty have been met or exceeded.   soilassociation.org

- **The Forest Stewardship Council** ensures that natural products – particularly wood-based products – are ethically sourced and responsibly managed.
                                fsc-uk.org/en-uk

- **Child Labor Free** is a US mark of commitment, particularly from clothing and fashion brands, to boycott supply chains that exploit child labour.
                                childlaborfree.com/site/get-accredited

- **Responsible 100** This mark shines a light on businesses seeking to be as socially, environmentally and ethically responsible as possible. Accredited companies need to submit a range of information about their values and business practices – and answer questions from community members.
                                responsible100.com

- **UTZ** This global accreditation scheme focuses on sustainable farming methods, particularly in coffee, cocoa, tea and nuts. It rewards those companies working towards a more sustainable world – 'better for the farmers, the workers, their families, the planet and all of us'.   utz.org

- **The Ecolabel Index** There are literally hundreds of different 'eco' labels and schemes across the globe – especially in the food and farming industries. The Ecolabel index website is perhaps the largest global directory – featuring over 450 different accreditation schemes. It's an excellent resource to find out about each ecological accreditation.   ecolabelindex.com

- **Rainforest Alliance** This non-profit, non-governmental organization works with farmers and landowners around the world to produce food, drink and consumer goods that conserve tropical forests. Its certification scheme shows a commitment to using sustainable business practices.
                    rainforest-alliance.org

Ethical awards

As companies increasingly accept (and want to shout about) their responsibilities to society and the environment, a range of awards has sprung up to celebrate their achievements.

From improving workers' rights to reducing carbon footprints, these showcase the most innovative, authentic and morally responsible businesses across every industry.

There is a note of warning. As with any claims of ethical intent, these kinds of award are only as credible as the organizations behind them – and the criteria their judges use.

Helpfully, one organization has already identified this problem – and created an accreditation scheme for ethical awards: the **RSA** (Royal Society for the encouragement of Arts, Manufactures and Commerce) Accreditation scheme identifies the most authentic ethical awards by providing a mark of quality to only those schemes that meet a robust set of criteria.   **rsaaccreditation.org**

It is also worth noting that the lists of some ethical award winners appear to be dominated by just those companies that you might think are the *least* morally responsible businesses. Transnational corporations, some of whom have even featured in high-profile human rights or environmental scandals, frequently scoop ethical awards for their corporate social responsibility or sustainability initiatives.

To understand why, you need to look at the awards themselves. And often, it's not as big a contradiction as it seems. Certainly, some awards are effectively 'greenwash' – a marketing exercise to spin some positive news about a business when the true picture is far less rosy. (For more on greenwash, see Page 132.) But frequently, large corporations are actually the very best places to find examples of outstanding sustainability initiatives in action.

One reason is that multi-million-dollar companies are in the rare and luxurious position of being able to invest huge sums of money (and therefore run vast projects and deliver incredible outcomes) when it comes to sustainability initiatives.

Depending on your moral position, this can be a problem. For example, if you're driven to work for an organization which is entirely committed to making a positive difference (and perhaps is widely recognized as a 'good guy'), you may shudder at the thought of joining one of these global giants. But if you're focused much more on impact – and potentially acting as the 'Trojan horse', as Anita Roddick once put it, these companies could be the perfect fit.

Don't be surprised, therefore, to see the likes of McDonald's, Shell and even British American Tobacco winning ethical awards. Typically, these will be for very specific initiatives (rather than for the whole business) – for example, how they report on their sustainability work.

The following list of awards isn't exhaustive, but you'll find many common ones here. By searching lists of current and previous winners, I hope you'll find plenty of inspiring companies to add to your potential employer list.

- **Ethical Corporation's Responsible Business Awards** These are widely recognized as one of the world's leading awards for CSR, sustainability, supply chain and business executives. They aim to recognize genuine, innovative and meaningful approaches to making responsible business a reality.

  events.ethicalcorp.com/awards/about.php

- **Business In The Community's Responsible Business Awards** These aim to capture and highlight 'inspiring stories of businesses as a positive force for change'. They are open to companies of any size, sector and scale, and entries are assessed and selected by over 250 business peers.

  bitc.org.uk/awards/responsible-business-awards

- **The Green Apple Environment Awards** Started by The Green Organisation in 1994, these are described as an 'annual international campaign to recognize, reward and promote environmental best practice around the world'. Their categories include Commerce and Industry, Built Environment and Architectural Heritage, and a special award for businesses based in Scotland.

  thegreenorganisation.info/green-apple-awards

- **Prince's Charities Tomorrow's Business Awards** This is a competition, supported by NatWest, for entrepreneurs who want to develop their business while making a positive difference to themselves, their local community or their environment.   princes-trust.org.uk/help-for-young-people/
  support-starting-business/tomorrows-business-awards

- **Third Sector's Business Charity Awards** These celebrate and highlight the great charity work of corporations in Britain. The Awards are open to any size of company in the UK, in any industry, that are involved in schemes to benefit charities or the voluntary sector. businesscharityawards.com

- **FT/IFC Transformational Business Awards** This is a collaboration between the *Financial Times* and global development institution the International Finance Corporation. The awards honour initiatives that provide innovative, commercially viable solutions to help improve lives and economies in developing countries. live.ft.com/Events/2016/
FT-IFC-Transformational-Business-Awards-and-Conference-2016

- **The Guardian's Sustainable Business Awards** From start-up of the year to unsung sustainability hero, The Guardian's annual awards are an excellent place to identify – and read more about – some of the most innovative and ethically minded businesses across the UK.
theguardian.com/sustainable-business/2016

- **Better Society Awards** These celebrate the efforts that commercial companies make in order to help create a better society. Organized by the Better Society Network, which also publishes *Charity Times* magazine, they honour businesses that have made a commitment to social, environmental and ethical impact. bettersociety.net/awards/index.php

- **Investors in People** These awards recognize the people and corporate teams that are making a positive impact on the world.
investorsinpeople.com/awards

- **edie sustainability leaders awards** Open to all businesses across the public and private sectors and of all sizes, these awards celebrate companies who show sustainability in their operations, business models and products.
awards.edie.net/2017/en/page/home

- **University Ethical Rankings** If you're thinking of pursuing an academic career, these alternative university rankings – from the UK's largest student campaigning network, People and Planet – will show you each institution's environmental and ethical performance, scored across 13 sustainability criteria. peopleandplanet.org/university-league

Arumza's choice

It is easy to assume that all transnationals simply don't care about the environment, or making a positive impact on the planet. But that's no truer than saying all small, family businesses are socially and environmentally responsible.

Your personal values may steer you towards working for a particular kind of business – but, for some people, large corporations can tick all of their ethical boxes, and enable them to contribute towards some incredible goals.

Arumza Rashid has experienced all of this, and firmly believes that big business isn't always bad. After quitting a prestigious graduate programme with one of the world's top four management consultants, she took a number of different career paths – driven largely by her own sense of values and ethics.

As sustainability programme manager for the technology division of the London Organising Committee for the Olympic Games (LOCOG), she devised and executed a plan to reduce the environmental impact of technology used at the London Olympics. This was part of an award-winning sustainability strategy for the 2012 Games.

Her subsequent (and most recent) role was contracting as Digital Project Manager at BP – focusing on global diversity and inclusion in technology. Here, she has helped oversee an increase in female representation in senior level positions by three per cent over two years. She has also helped to develop an innovative social enterprise for girls aged nine and over. Called Modern Muse, this mobile app gives young girls direct access to female role models in the science, technology, engineering and maths industries.

Here Arumza talks about her career in sustainability and diversity, and shares some of the lessons she has learned along the way.

Lots of us are looking for change

I often see people working at companies and can tell how unhappy they are. They want to do something different, but there's a fear. How do I get a(nother) job?

I understand that. I was working at KPMG but, after two years, I realized I wasn't getting any personal satisfaction.

Who leaves one of the 'Big Four' global consultancy firms that early in their career?

Take risks

I don't spend time pondering. It was a risk to leave KPMG – especially as

I resigned without having another job. I was 23. But I think it's easier to take a risk when you're younger. I didn't have to think about mortgages. There weren't any other people relying on me.

Making a difference

I wanted to do something that transparently made a difference to people's lives. I came across an ad for the Met Police, looking for people to help improve the service through technology. It was a massive pay cut – they couldn't understand why I wanted to do it. But it was the best four years of my career.

If I feel like I'm not making a difference, I switch off. If you follow what you believe in, based on values, I think the money can follow. You have to be realistic, though. At one point, I needed to think about my standard of living – and I took a freelance role at the Ambulance Service, which was paid better, as I was a contractor.

Seize your opportunities

When I went to work (as programme manager for sustainability and diversity in technology) at the Olympics, it was really badly paid – and I made that choice deliberately. I knew I wouldn't get that kind of opportunity again.

Sometimes luck also comes into it. After the London Games, I could have gone travelling. But I made sure I got out there. I gave a technology talk about delivering sustainable games and was spotted by a female CIO. We talked about the gender imbalance at that conference, and she heard I was out of a job. That's what led to my joining BP.

Walking the talk

Lots of people think an oil company like BP is just ruining the environment. And everyone can have their view. But I think you also have to look at the sustainability of an oil and gas company: what are they trying to do to help the community? I stayed at BP because they didn't just talk about it, they invested in it – they meant what they said.

My advice

When you're early in your career, take the leap because it's a lot easier to do it then. You've got less to lose. You don't always have to have the plan. That's been my career story.

Not following a linear career path is great because you can end up with a sequence of jobs that might take you in any direction.

Later in your career, you do have to think of other factors, such as: how long am I willing to do this for? You may need to have a short-term plan financially.

These days I find that I increasingly fall back on my networks and career sponsors whom I've met along the way. It's important to build your own reputation because no-one else will do it – and you'd be surprised where reputation can get you.

Online communities

If you want to find the people behind ethically minded businesses, there are many more places to look than kitemarks and awards.

You will find dozens of useful resources, communities, news sites and forums on the web, which can help you to identify potential employers and roles – and connect with the people who can help you.

Some of these are sector-specific, others more general. Some have jobs boards, others are more about networking or giving you inspiration for your next move.

The following list isn't exhaustive but it should help you find interesting communities and networks in the areas that most interest you.

Education

- **Teach First** is a charity providing leadership programmes specifically for education. Its mission is to end educational inequality by finding, training and supporting people to become brilliant teachers – inspiring the young people who need them the most. They have an active online community where you'll find opportunities, news, local activities and events.   teachfirst.org.uk

Fashion

- **The Ethical Fashion Forum SOURCE Network** is an online fashion community dedicated to sustainability – bringing together thousands of members, from fashion designers to press, buyers, students, entrepreneurs, consumers and businesspeople in over 100 countries. Through this network they regularly promote ethical-fashion job, internship and funding opportunities to their members.   ethicalfashionforum.com

Science, Engineering and Technology

- **Data Kind UK** is an active community of volunteers and changemakers who use data analysis to help social change. Its UK chapter holds regular meetups where you'll encounter other conscientious dataists and tech-savvy social innovators doing great things. Their Meetup page has details of their activities and a discussion board where job opportunities are often posted.

  meetup.com/datakind-uk
  datakind.org/chapters/datakind-uk

- **Institution of Mechanical Engineers** has a special interest group – The Energy, Environment and Sustainability Group (EESG) – with over 20,000 members. The EESG is 'the natural intellectual home for engineers who want to learn about sustainability engineering' and they regularly hold seminars, exhibitions and debates – a great opportunity to get involved with the sustainable engineering community. Their main website also has excellent job-hunting resources for mechanical-engineering careers in general.

  imeche.org/get-involved/special-interest-groups/
  energy-environment-and-sustainability-group

- **NetSquared** is an international community that brings together nonprofits, activists, tech leaders, funders, and everyone who's interested in using technology for social change. The NetSquared London chapter runs monthly meetups for local members to come together to share ideas, ask questions, network, and collaborate around using technology for social benefit.

  meetup.com/netsquaredlondon/

- **Royal Academy of Engineering (RAE)** This holds regular talks, events and networking opportunities for engineers all over the world. Engineering a Better World is an annual two-day event that explores how engineering can drive progress towards the UN's Sustainable Development Goals. RAE also provides grants and fellowships to budding engineering entrepreneurs.

  raeng.org.uk/engineeringabetterworld

- **Scientists for Global Responsibility (SGR)** is an independent UK-based membership organization of hundreds of natural scientists, social scientists, engineers, IT professionals and architects. They promote science, design and technology that contribute to peace, social justice and environmental sustainability by holding regular events, creating publications and running research projects. Their Ethical Careers project resulted in a number of helpful publications, presentations and articles, as well as a contact list of ethical employers in the sector.
  sgr.org.uk/projects/ethical-careers

- **Tech for Good** exists to tell the stories of the people and technology making the world a better place. It aims to build a Tech for Good community through holding events, promoting jobs and sharing the latest research, news and insights. Try its job listings board for the latest opportunities in impactful tech careers – in the UK and internationally.
  techforgood.global/jobs

Environment, conservation and animal welfare

- **Countryside Jobs Service (CJS)** is an active site providing volunteering, training and job opportunities in the countryside, conservation and ecology – including wildlife work and environmental education.

  countryside-jobs.com

- **EnvironmentJob.co.uk** has hundreds of advertisers and 63,000 subscribers making it the 'UK's busiest environmental job site'. You'll find opportunities across the UK including roles in wildlife conservation, ecology, sustainability, farming, climate and energy. environmentjob.co.uk

- *Permaculture* is a quarterly green and environmental magazine – available both digitally and in print. As well as features and news from around the world, the magazine also includes contributions, tips and advice from its readers. You'll find eco-based job opportunities in its classified ads section. permaculture.co.uk/classifieds

Corporate Social Responsibility (CSR), sustainability and built environment

- **2degrees** is an online platform bringing together people and businesses across the globe so that they can solve sustainability issues. The 2degrees community page is open to all and its members can access job opportunities, webinars, insights, resources, and even ask the community a question or set it a challenge. 2degreesnetwork.com/groups/2degrees-community

- **Acre** is a recruitment agency focused on careers in sustainability, corporate responsibility, environment, health & safety and energy. acre.com

- **Allen & York** is a recruitment agency that specializes in recruiting for jobs in CSR, social impact, environmental management, sustainable supply chain and corporate sustainability. allen-york.com

- **edie** This is a sizeable portal of news, commentary, advice and tools for sustainability professionals. Its aim is to provide people with the information and resources they need to do business better. Although it's aimed at existing sustainability employees, you'll find lots of useful advice, networking events and a small jobs board. edie.net

- *Ethical Corporation* This digital and print magazine provides business intelligence and advice. Its target market is organizations looking to be more responsible – through CSR, compliance, risk and governance communities, and you'll also find a jobs board.   ethicalcorp.com/jobs

- **Ethical Performance** This provides news, features and reports on corporate social responsibility and socially responsible investing. The media group incorporates a website and a CSR services directory as well as a newsletter for senior executives and SRI personnel and a bi-monthly magazine. The site also has a jobs board.

  ethicalperformance.com
  ethicalperformance.com/directory
  ethicalperformance.com/recruitment

- **Evergreen Resources** is a recruitment company specializing in environmental and built-environment careers – including Energy, Waste Management, Engineering, Redevelopment, Sustainability and CSR.

  evergreen.org.uk

- **GreenJobs.co.uk** A jobs board for 'green experts', this includes hundreds of environment-focused roles in the private and public sectors – from architects and engineers to waste managers and energy experts.   greenjobs.co.uk

- **Walk of Life** Run by careers consultant Shannon Houde, this is the first international career advisory service focused solely on the sustainability, social impact, international development and Corporate Responsibility sectors. Her blog contains a wealth of information for job seekers and she regularly posts details of the latest 'Hot Jobs'.

  walkoflifeconsulting.com/category/hot-jobs

Finance and investment

- **The UK Sustainable Investment and Finance Association** is the membership association for sustainable and responsible financial services. It promotes responsible investment and other forms of finance that support sustainable economic development, enhance quality of life and safeguard the environment. They occasionally post career opportunities in their jobs section and have regular events and conferences.

  uksif.org

Healthcare

- **The Centre for Sustainable Healthcare** has active networks dedicated to sustainability in various parts of the healthcare sector including dentistry, mental health, occupational therapy, operating theatres and primary care. They regularly hold events and share news and resources.

  networks.sustainablehealthcare.org.uk

Law

- **The Charity Law Association** has over 900 members, including charity advisers, charity professionals, academics and those with experience and knowledge of how charities operate. As a member you can attend meetings with speakers who are leaders in the field, discuss issues with your peers, receive regular updates and contribute to the development of law and policy. If you're interested in a career in charity law, this could be a valuable way to network.

  charitylawassociation.org.uk

- **The Law Society's Human Rights Community** runs a programme for solicitors and students interested in human rights. As a member, you can join their International Action Team, attend events and training, engage with them on policy issues and receive their monthly updates – which include volunteering and job opportunities.

  communities.lawsociety.org.uk/human-rights/
  get-involved/law-society-programmes

Start-ups and entrepreneurs

- **The Skoll Foundation** This organization's mission is to drive large-scale change by investing in, connecting and celebrating social entrepreneurs and innovators who help them solve the world's most pressing problems. They have a thriving global community, hold events and workshops, and have a jobs board covering unique opportunities in the NGO, government and CSR sectors.

  skoll.org/community/jobs

- **Work In Start-ups** Many start-ups want to improve the world through their innovation – and they need like-minded employees. But how can you find these companies when they're still mostly unknown? Work In Start-ups is a jobs board filled with start-up job opportunities, including marketing, design, testing, customer service and web/software development.

  workinstartups.com

"It's not how much money that ultimately makes us happy between nine and five. It's whether or not our work fulfils us."

Malcolm Gladwell

Graduates and young people

- **Change agents** is a not-for-profit recruitment agency aiming to create a network of people who are 'empowered to live and work in a way that makes a positive impact on the world around them'. They specialize in recruiting and developing graduates and young people for ethical careers.

  changeagents.org.uk

- **The Cool Graduate** believes: 'There is not enough support out there for the moment when you fall off the university conveyor belt. We're starting a careers advice revolution.' Set up by graduates, for graduates, they've compiled resources to help you find meaningful careers around the world.

  thecoolgraduate.com

More inspiration

- **OneWorld** is a charity focused on innovating new media, mobile and web technologies for social good, helping people across the world to improve their lives. Their jobs section includes the latest employment and volunteering opportunities from organizations working to create a better world.

  oneworld.org/jobs

- **EcoJam** This Bristol-based website aims to foster everything green and ethical in the UK. Find a directory of ethical businesses and organizations, events, news, volunteering opportunities and job roles.   **ecojam.org/bristol**

- **Elevator Café** call themselves 'The Good Job Network' because they only promote jobs with social enterprises, charities and purpose-driven companies. You can create a profile as a job-seeker or freelancer so that ethical employers can find you, sign up for job alerts via email, and follow their Facebook or Twitter feeds for the latest news and opportunities.   **elevatorcafe.com**

- **Escape The City** runs programmes specifically for people who want to find meaningful careers and put purpose before profit. It has an active global community of like-minded people and its opportunities page is regularly updated with job and internship listings from businesses and organizations across the UK and the rest of the world.   **escapethecity.org/opportunities**

- *Ethical Consumer* As the name suggests, this website, magazine and guide is primarily focused upon goods and services but also has a large directory of brands and businesses which it scores on a number of ethical criteria. It also maintains a directory of ethical pressure groups and runs its own campaigns and boycotts.

ethicalconsumer.org

LinkedIn networks

As well as countless job listings, LinkedIn also has many groups and networks of people who are focused on having meaningful careers and making the world a better place. Here are just a couple:

- **UK Green Jobs & Career Network**: A resource to help people looking for work in social or environmental responsibility.

  linkedin.com/groups/2890848/profile

- **Conservation Jobs – Careers & Talent Network**: A forum for conservation professionals to connect and discuss all aspects of the conservation industry.

  linkedin.com/groups/4141692/profile

Dodging the greenwash

In recent years, many companies have realized that we – both as consumers and employees – like businesses that care about people and planet. Given the choice, we prefer to shop with, and work for, companies that make a difference – so there's actually a strong *commercial* reason to appear ethical.

The key word here is 'appear' – as, for some businesses, it's really smoke and mirrors. Greenwashing is when companies falsely claim to be socially or environmentally responsible. According to the site greenwashingindex – which identifies some of the main offenders – it's 'whitewashing with a 'green' brush'.

How can you spot greenwash? One approach is to look at the company as a whole. Are their environmental credentials displayed proudly on their site, or hidden away? Do their awards and accreditations come from reputable organizations?

greenwashingindex.com

In its 'Behind the Label' series, *The Ecologist* magazine (**theecologist.org**) highlights numerous examples of questionable business practices. Here's just one example:

L'Oréal is currently the world's biggest cosmetics brand. And arguably its most outspoken critic, says *The Ecologist*, is animal welfare campaign group Naturewatch, which has long called for a boycott of all L'Oréal products (including those sold by The Body Shop). Naturewatch claims that the company still uses animal testing extensively.

L'Oréal disputes this – saying that it has not tested any of its 'finished products' on animals since 1989. It's a complicated debate – but whichever organization you believe, you certainly won't find any of this on L'Oréal's website (**loreal.com**).

Here, you're far more likely to read articles entitled 'One of the most ethical companies in the world' – which explains how the 'Ethisphere Institute' has bestowed this honour on L'Oréal no less than five times.

'Because it is fundamental for our success to obtain results with respect and integrity, L'Oréal puts ethics at the heart of its strategy,' says Emmanuel Lulin, Senior Vice-President & Chief Ethics Officer of L'Oréal. 'Our ethical principles of Integrity, Respect, Courage and Transparency are always upheld wherever we operate in the world, any time we make a decision, big or small.'

So who is telling the truth? In some cases, it's clear when a company's marketing department is spinning us a fabrication. But sometimes it's very hard to tell. Ethics are personal, and there can be lots of grey areas. Even an incredibly sustainable company like Patagonia (see Page 111) says it's not a perfect model of an ethical business: 'We don't do everything a responsible company can do, nor does anyone else we know,' says its founder.

What matters most is that you believe in a business and can see that it's making a positive difference – not just constructing an ethical story to sell more products. You can do some research from afar, but if you get to interview stage with a company, it is a great opportunity to check if they're truly walking the talk.

Susan Camberis is HR Director at Baxter Healthcare Corporation. Talking to ethical business network, Net Impact, she recommends using the fact that you'll meet with more than one person at an organization to ask the exact same sustainability question.

'Compare the answers you get,' she says, 'and you'll be better able to understand how committed the company really is to working on the issue(s) by gauging how well its employees can communicate its sustainability efforts.' **baxter.com**

Going it alone

This isn't a business start-up book – and we don't have space to cover every aspect of creating an ethical company from scratch. But as you explore your future careers, you may decide – now or later on – to work for yourself.

Whether that means freelancing, taking on contract work or setting up your own business, there are many different routes that can put you in control.

You will find many inspiring examples of people who have left school or university and immediately set up a successful ethically minded business. But from my research, at least, it seems that most people who get it right will have two things in common.

First, they'll have gained some experience first hand, often within a very ordinary business setting. If nothing else, this gives them a benchmark for 'business as usual', and more typically it's a brilliant way to learn what to do – and what not to do. (For example, read Neal Gershinson's story on Page 97). Second, they have learned from their mistakes.

Let's meet two people who have furrowed their own unique career paths.

Jocelyn's advice

Jocelyn Whipple is a sustainable fashion consultant and a pioneer in the global ethical fashion movement. She worked for fashion brands, and was tempted to set up her own label, before taking a change of direction. She realized that the world 'didn't need' another ethical fashion line, but it did need someone fighting the corner of the sustainable fashion movement.

Jocelyn reflects on her career, and shares some advice for ethical job seekers.

Think 'together'

When you're working with an established industry like fashion, I don't think it's helpful to disassociate an 'ethical' sector from the mainstream as it's then an uphill battle: it's you against us. For me, it's not separate; it's a way of working within the industry. There isn't an ethical fashion contingent of NGOs telling the fashion industry how things should be – any change is coming from individuals, and that includes new graduates who are arriving with a new mindset.

I needed to ask questions...

I studied design and making – and because of my personal ethics and outlook on life, I began to ask questions. I wanted to know where my materials were coming from, how I was contributing to society in a bigger way. That's really how the wider ethical fashion movement was formed.

... and find like-minded people

I didn't know what I wanted to be when I grew up. I did a Btec, went to university and then found my focus in material and textile sustainability. There weren't any jobs for that then – but I found a community who were passionate about the same thing.

I've gone through phases

I was an employee for fashion companies – and took that industry experience into my own business as sole trader. I focused on what I felt the industry needed most. It didn't need me creating another brand. So I concentrated on helping existing [ethical] brands get into shops.

Looking beyond

It's important not to get trapped in what you think a role or job title is. Look for careers that don't necessarily exist but you think are needed. There's always a need for innovation, and industry can

135

potentially solve things that NGOs, think tanks and academics can't.

As a consultant...

I don't think there's anyone I wouldn't work with. It comes back to the idea of working within the existing industry. There are always opportunities for things to be done differently and it's better to be on the inside. When I started, people said wouldn't it be amazing if Topshop had organic cotton – and now they do. Whatever [you think of them] there is a sense of achievement that this change has happened. Participating in systems is key to wanting to make change. Unless we do that we're just plodding along – we're not changing anything.

Balance matters

Work-life balance is crucial for me. It's liberating when you realize that you don't have to slot into a specific career. I now live in the mountains in southern Spain. I work from home, close to the person I adore, and I choose my own hours. That balance is important for my sense of purpose in the world. I realized early on that no-one was going to provide that for me, and I had to define it myself.

The best advice I've had

In 1999 I became friends with someone who had a market stall selling beaded bracelets, which he made himself. He'd done it for several years and had saved a deposit, got a mortgage and was making a decent living from his craft. He encouraged me to get a licence for my own stall and start selling what I was making (bags and hats and small items from recently developed organic cotton and hemp fabrics).

His first piece of advice was for me to register as self-employed and to sign up for a free tax class. It only lasted a few hours, and I came away feeling informed, empowered and confident. It opened up and demystified my right to know and to actively make use of labour laws and opportunities. Since then I have been almost exclusively self-employed and I've never been afraid to access whatever information I need from government in order to operate my business. It has provided me with self-responsibility and account-ability as a sort of 'mast' for whatever the focus of my work has been and it's something I value greatly and don't take for granted.

My advice for ethical career seekers

Don't think of your more 'ethical career' as something separate or different or other than your existing work. Rather look with honesty and curiosity at your existing role and the industry you work in and start to identify the 'hows', 'wheres' and 'whys' it can be practised more 'ethically'. Take hold of those ideas for change and make them your own. Try them out, find the other people in your industry who are doing the same thing, connect with them to support each other to create change from within. And don't forget to share information with wider society about what needs changing.

Freelancing

There are many ways that you can shape your career without taking on a full-time position. One of the upsides of part-time, contract or freelance work is that it enables you to try out a variety of roles and areas without too much commitment.

This can help you understand what it's like to work in a particular field, discover where your heart really lies, and identify the areas that you want to specialize in – or avoid.

Caspar's journey

For **Caspar van Vark**, pursuing a career with purpose has involved some calculated moves, a leap of faith – and a growing understanding of what really matters to him.

I started out in magazine production

It was a large publishing company, and it was fun for a while. But it became very predictable. On a Monday in January, I knew exactly what I'd be doing on the same day in August...

When I quit, I started freelancing

I began writing about charities for *Third Sector* magazine. A pivotal moment was moving into a shared freelance office with other writers and designers, and a communications agency with many charity clients. I started getting a lot of copywriting work from them, and it was great to have a desk in a cool office.

After a while, I realized that I needed to be more proactive in steering my own career – I couldn't just be the person who stepped in when other people had too much work.

Finding a niche

In 2008, I was reading a lot about food issues. It was the time of the global food price crisis, which affected millions of people – and it really struck a chord. And I was already thinking that I needed to specialize: it wasn't enough just to be a 'charity writer'.

I found a part-time, two-year Masters degree in Food Policy at City University. Looking back, it was a major decision – but it happened very fast. I read about it in August and started in September. I just knew it was the right thing to do.

A big break

My lucky break happened as I was finishing my dissertation. *The Guardian* newspaper launched a new global development section, which included a subsection on food and agriculture in the developing world. I remember sitting in the British Library when that email came through. I'd written a few features for *The Guardian* before – and, over the next few years, I was able to build up a body of work on a specialist subject area. And that opened up doors with various NGOs, who wanted me to work for them.

But I soon hit a point when freelancing wasn't really helping me any more. As a journalist, I always felt slightly on the outside. Now I wanted to be the expert – and to actually make more of a difference.

Slower can be better

Today I'm running the All Party Parliamentary Group on Food and Agriculture for Development, which is based at the House of Lords. The role is funded by a dozen NGOs, and the aim is to help politicians understand the issues faced by smallholder farmers in the developing world, and why it matters to us. Ultimately, it's about addressing hunger and malnutrition.

It's a very different pace. As a freelance journalist, you might have one week jetting off to report on a story and see your article published. But the next week you could be at home, your story is yesterday's news, and no-one's interested in your next idea.

Now it's a slower process – but I'm chipping away, and helping to make real change happen, rather than just writing about it. I find that more satisfying.

Making an impact

Am I making a difference? Not every day, no. But I feel that I'm working on something that matters – and that's fulfilling enough for me. I'm glad that I'm now truly part of a sector that I care about.

Looking back, I wonder if I did it the wrong way round. If I re-entered freelance life now, I'd have much more expertise behind me. I think there's a good argument for developing that specialist knowledge first, and freelancing afterwards.

My advice...

...for anyone looking to pursue an ethical career is to keep making decisions. If you think you know what you want to do, even taking a small step is important. You just need to keep moving in the right direction.

I also feel you shouldn't put too much pressure on yourself to keep looking for the next opportunity. There's a sense that everything has to be a career springboard nowadays, but if you're doing something that you enjoy – just enjoy it.

Whatever you decide to do next, it's important to note that there are options beyond the regular 9-to-5 routine.

But, of course, if you do want to join a company – or are currently feeling trapped in a role that isn't aligned to your ethics – there are lots of ways to add meaning and purpose to the 'daily grind'.

And that's what the next section is all about.

Be an intrapreneur

If you want to find a fulfilling job that can help change the world, it's not just a choice between going it alone, or getting a job with a charity or an ethically minded company.

In recent years, an increasingly powerful movement has been growing across the world – and it's being driven by a group of extraordinary employees within very ordinary companies.

Some people call them 'cubicle warriors', or 'corporate change-makers', but the most common nickname is 'intrapreneurs'.

From the inside

Intrapreneurs harness corporate power as a force for good. These are regular employees within companies (often major corporations), who think up and promote practical solutions to social or environmental challenges – and get those companies to put their ideas into practice. In short, they're looking to improve 'business as usual' from the inside.

From better environmental performance to pioneering projects that help disadvantaged people, there is no limit to the kind of change that an intrapreneur can influence. The good news is that the number of companies that have realized the value of listening to their employees' ideas and dreams for a better world is growing. And many of them are major employers.

> **Defining an intrapreneur**
>
> 'An intrapreneur acts like an entrepreneur within a larger organization. He or she tends to be highly self-motivated, proactive and action-oriented – comfortable with taking the initiative, even within the boundaries of an organzation, in pursuit of an innovative product or service.'
>
> *Investopedia*

Take Sam McCracken, who was working in Nike's warehouse in the US state of Oregon. As a member of the Native American Sioux people, he knew about the chronic obesity and diabetes that was affecting his community – and started to think about what his employer could do to help. He shared his ideas, and – over the next few years – that concept grew into an entire business unit for Nike called N7. Its mission is to inspire Native American and Aboriginal young people to participate in sport and physical activity.

This is funded by sales of N7 products, which include a unique model of performance shoe that meets the specific fit and width requirements for the Native American foot. It's a successful product for Nike, and is addressing important social and health needs in an otherwise disenfranchised community.

One of the best-known – and most successful – examples of social intrapreneur-ship is Vodafone's M-Pesa programme, which was dreamed up by employee Nick Hughes. He realized that millions of Africans didn't have access to computers – and were therefore struggling to access valuable financial products and services. And he wanted his employer, Vodafone, to do something about it.

The Intrapreneur's Toolkit

Among the many helpful (and well-written) resources that you'll find on the League of Intrapreneurs website is a guide called the Intrapreneur's Toolkit. This includes 10 top pieces of advice to help you hit the ground running. We've paraphrased them below:

1 Target the pain points
What are your company's pain points? How do they get measured and what are their performance indicators?

2 Make it stick
People can only process so much information, and many already feel over-loaded. So amidst meeting notes, agendas, emails and Power Point presentations, how do you really get your message to stick?

3 Connect with corporate priorities
Scan your CEO's statements or other corporate PR for publicly declared vision, mission and projects.

4 Be authentic
Human beings have a finely tuned bullshit detector. As a result, much of the art of persuasion boils down to being authentic.

5 Back up your hunch with evidence
Hunches rank too high on the PWI (the 'Perceived Weirdness Index').

That idea became the product M-Pesa, which today enables millions of people (many of whom don't have bank accounts or local branches) to deposit, withdraw, transfer money and pay for goods and services easily using a mobile phone. As well as kickstarting a trend in mobile money systems, M-Pesa has grown and is now used in countries from Afghanistan and India to Albania. It has been praised for giving millions of previously excluded people access to a formal financial system, and for reducing crime in otherwise largely cash-based societies.

And this amazing global change started with just one employee's idea for a fairer world.

It will appeal to true believers but isolate the majority. Hunches backed by evidence de-risk the proposal.

6 Practise your pitch
Practice makes perfect. But don't practise your story or pitch in isolation.

7 Find partners to share
This is about risk (and opportunity). No-one wants to take 100 per cent of the risk. Find someone to share the risk and watch your company breathe a sigh of relief.

8 Listen
Listening is the cornerstone of empathy. Take time to listen to people and understand their needs, priorities and motivations.

9 Guard against mission drift
We've all heard of great-sounding initiatives that get watered down by corporate priorities. Be clear from the start about your initiative's non-negotiables and don't compromise on these.

10 Speak your audience's language
A key skill for social intrapreneurs is 'code switching' or knowing how to speak the language of your audience.

Adapted from The Intrapeneur's Toolkit © the League of Intrapreneurs.

What Sam at Nike and Nick at Vodafone realized is that it's possible to be heard, even at a transnational. A common metaphor for global corporations is that they're 'tankers' in the ocean – in other words, it is hard work and takes a long time to get them to change direction. But if you can succeed, thanks to their size and reach the effects can be astonishing .

This focus on 'impact' is at the heart of the pioneering careers advice organization **80,000 hours**. Its mantra is that you have a limited amount of time to make a positive difference – and that means every hour counts. To put it crudely, why work for a small community business (where you might affect the lives of a few dozen people in your neighbourhood) when you could work for a giant corporation and change the world? If you're interested in delivering the biggest social impact for your time and effort, it's definitely worth exploring the excellent 80,000 hours website.

80000hours.org

In some ways, this notion of employees trying to make a positive difference is nothing new. We have been improving the way that businesses run, from the inside, for hundreds of years. However, the current 'social intrapreneurship' movement started to really gain momentum in 2013, when entrepreneurs Richard Branson and Guy Kawasaki began to talk about it – and when the League of Intrapreneurs was founded.

Billed as 'a global movement of corporate changemakers working to transform business from the inside out', the League of Intrapreneurs was started by Ashoka – a global organization committed to finding the most cutting-edge social-change agents – and management consultancy firm Accenture.

Today, it is the go-to resource for would-be intrapreneurs – filled with ideas, advice and tips for employees around the globe.

leagueofintrapreneurs.com

What can you affect?

How can intrapreneurs make a difference? In truth, the only limitation is your imagination – it simply depends how you want to make your mark.

For an overview of the main kinds of opportunity for ethically minded employees, here is think tank SustainAbility's top 10 list of 'divides and opportunities' for intrapreneurs.

Divides	Realities	Opportunities
1 **Demographic**	The world is heading to a population of 9 billion by 2050 with 95% of growth expected in developing countries.	To meet the needs of billions of people affected by market failures in both developing and developed countries.
2 **Financial**	40% of the world's wealth is owned by 1% of the population while the poorest 50% can claim just 1% of the wealth.	Help the have-nots become bankable, insurable and entrepreneurial.
3 **Nutritional**	The world now produces enough food for everyone, but over 850 million people still face chronic hunger every day.	Address the needs of those with too little food – and too much.
4 **Resources**	60% of the ecosystem services, such as fresh water and climate regulation, are being degraded or used unsustainably.	Enable development that uses the earth's resources in a sustainable way.
5 **Environmental**	The loss of biodiversity, droughts, and the destruction of coral reefs are just some of the challenges facing the globe.	Create markets that protect and enhance the environment.
6 **Health**	Some 39.5 million people live with HIV/AIDS in the world, now the fourth-largest killer disease.	Create markets that encourage healthy lifestyles and enable equal access to healthcare.
7 **Gender**	Two-thirds of the world's 1 billion illiterate people are women.	Enable and empower women to participate equally and fairly in society and the economy.
8 **Educational**	About 100 million children within emerging economies are not enrolled in primary education.	Provide the mechanisms to transfer and share knowledge and learning that empower all levels of societies.
9 **Digital**	Internet users worldwide topped 1.1 billion in 2007, but only 4% of Africans and 11% of Asians have internet access.	Develop inclusive technology that enables all levels of society to tackle each of these divides more effectively.
10 **Security**	Between 1994 and 2004, most of the 13 million deaths caused by intra-state conflict took place in sub-Saharan Africa and western and southern Asia	Work to promote security and reduce conflict based on inequality and exclusion.

Adapted from *Raising our Game: Can We Sustain Globalization?* © SustainAbility

Getting started

We don't have space here to detail everything you could do to change a company from within – and, besides, that book already exists.

Although it's written from a US perspective, Gerald F Davis and Christopher J White's book *Changing Your Company from the Inside Out* presents an in-depth roadmap for would-be intrapreneurs, covering important areas such as how to read your company's willingness to change and time your move, how to sell your idea into the business and find the right people to make a successful team, and how to get everyone supporting your initiative once you've launched.

Here's an excerpt that shows the potential impact that even very junior staff can achieve at a major corporation:

'Shortly after accounting giants Price Waterhouse and Coopers & Lybrand merged in 1998, a pair of young interns based in London – Amy Middleberg from the United States and New Zealander James Shaw – were asked their thoughts on what kind of values should guide the newly christened PriceWaterhouseCoopers (PwC). They took the challenge seriously and proposed a triple-bottom-line business that measured not just financial performance but social and environmental performance as well.

'Moreover, they believed that PwC could begin by creating a social audit that drew on the accounting firm's core competencies and that could serve clients aiming to track their own performance. With the audacity of youth, they recruited an ally, Fabio Sgaragli, who had joined the firm to work on merger integration.

'They also boldly managed to convince Jermyn Brooks, a global managing partner, of the merits of their idea. This in turn led to meetings with other important influencers in the new company; each received a customized pitch... and the three rapidly managed to be named as team leads for the project. Despite being relatively inexperienced and unconnected in the new organization, they were able to take their proposal forward.'

Today, 'sustainability services' are a hugely important business focus for PwC across the globe. The firm now helps companies develop corporate social responsibility and sustainability strategies, which help organizations understand and improve their social, environmental and economic impact.

Building career capital

Even though we've seen some inspiring examples of junior members of staff making a huge difference to the biggest companies, that's not always how it goes. In fact, it can be hard for inexperienced job seekers even to get a foot in the door at organizations where they'd like to make a difference.

The Catch 22 is that you need to show some experience and expertise to impress, but you can't gain that without someone giving you the opportunity.

The answer for many people is something called **career capital**. This is essentially a strategy for getting to a position of influence as quickly as possible.

Laura Vanderkam, author of the US ebook series *What the Most Successful People Do at Work*, defines career capital as 'the sum total of your experiences, your knowledge, your skills, your relationships'. She believes that all these things enable you to get a new job if you need one, create new situations for yourself or other people, or even let you take a break without having it ruin your career.

Talking to Forbes.com, she notes that successful people 'tend to pay in to their career capital account regularly' and there are three main ways to do this:

- One is to improve existing skills or learn new ones. This could mean taking professional development classes, or finding a mentor to help you understand what you'll need to learn to succeed in future.

- Her second tip is to develop a portfolio of your work. This is all about making your work visible – whether that means creating a physical portfolio or being able to show your impact another way.

- Her final idea to build your career capital is to build up a network of people loyal to you. This is as much about giving as taking – and Vanderkam recommends giving references to other people and introducing them to people you know who could help in their careers. It's all about creating a group based on loyalty and trust.

If you're looking to pursue a career with purpose, keep this concept of career capital in mind. Whether you're looking for a new job, or seeking to make a change within an existing role, it can help increase your chances of being heard and making a difference.

One approach to building up career capital, which ticks all of Vanderkam's boxes, is **volunteering**. Done right, it can be an excellent way to simultaneously learn valuable new skills, create a measurable portfolio of achievements, and find like-minded people willing to help one another.

The advantages of volunteering also apply to finding work in the charity sector – in fact, perhaps even more so than for corporate roles. It shows you are proactive, committed to a cause, and are motivated by more than money.

How do you find the right volunteer roles to build up your career capital? Few of us can afford to give up too much time without being paid, and that means you need to make any time spent volunteering count.

The next chapter is focused on just that. Let's explore how volunteering could help you take the next step in your career.

Give your time

Volunteering

SA

ДУРЫН

САЙН

GÖNÜLLÜ

VOLON

VRIJWILLIGER

VOLUNTARIO

FREIWILLIGE

AN

NGUYỄN

VOLONTARIUSZ

BRIVPRATĪGAIS

BRĪVPRATĪGAIS

TSITRAPO MAGBOLUNTARYO

VOLONTÄR

VOLUNTÁR

VOLA

Image to go here

DOBROVOLNÍK

VOLUNTÁRIO

VOLUNTÁRIO

VOLUNTÁRIO

PROSTOWOLSEJ

BÉNÉVOLE

SUKARELAWAN

VOLUNTEER

ΕΘΕΛΟΝΤΗΣ

MAGBOLUNTARYO

ZOKUZITHANDELA

ボランティア

VOLONTÄR

ΟΡΥ

ΕΘΕΛΟΝΤΗΣ

志愿者

ЧUUU

स्वयंसेवक

ВОЛОНТЕР

FRIVILLIG

DEONACH

KAI

ÖNKÉNT

OFUFO

داوطلب

স্বেচ্ছাসেবক

TÌNH

AFỌ

KUJITOLEA

Give your time

From the people working for charities and other ethical organizations (the Doers) to those demonstrating that for-profit businesses can also have a positive impact on the world (the Changers), we have met dozens of inspiring individuals in this book.

Over the course of my career, I have interviewed hundreds of employees and entrepreneurs who have successfully found work that they love. And the single most common piece of careers advice they've shared is one simple word: volunteer.

In the charity and social-enterprise sector, it is almost a given. How better to prove that you care about issues beyond money than freely to give your time to a good cause?

But this is just as true in the private sector. Countless surveys over the past few years – from expert groups including youth-volunteering organization Vinspired and The Institute for Volunteering Research – have revealed the benefits that volunteering can bring to future careers. These show that potential employers, even in the corporate world, feel that volunteering is an excellent way to help people advance their careers, with many believing that candidates with volunteering experience are more motivated than others.

But how easy is it to use volunteering as a stepping-stone into a paid role? Unless you choose carefully, you could spend a lot of time and effort doing unpaid work – but not benefiting your career. And if you can only volunteer for a limited time, it's even more important to make every opportunity count.

In this chapter, we'll take a look at effective volunteering for an ethical career.

Why volunteer?

'The most powerful way to prove you can do the work is to actually do some of it. Doing the work is the best way to figure out whether you're good at it, so it'll help you to avoid wasting your own time too.'

80,000 hours.org

There are plenty of great reasons for volunteering – and many are purely altruistic. But it's also true that giving your time can be an excellent springboard into employment.

In recent years, the Institute for Volunteering Research (IVR) has looked at this link, and found that some kinds of volunteering can be very effective at leading directly to paid jobs. For example, it reports that over 80 per cent of the full-time volunteers involved with the National Trust move on to employment or further training.

Their note of caution is that volunteering isn't a 'magic wand'. There's never a guarantee that it'll open up paid opportunities – but there are many things you can do to increase the chances.

What you get (when you give)

Volunteering can help you to move towards your dream career in many different ways. Here are just a few:

Confidence and self-esteem: If you're just starting out or making a career switch into a new area, self-belief is incredibly important. If you can't convince yourself that you're totally ready to take on the role, you may struggle to inspire others. Volunteering is an excellent, low-risk way to prove your ability and credentials – as much to yourself as to anyone else.

Soft skills: When they're asked about the career benefits of volunteering, employers typically focus on two things: a candidate's ability to work in a team and to communicate effectively. These 'softer' employment skills may not be specific to any particular role, but they're an incredibly important part of most jobs. Volunteering can also help you develop many more soft skills – from being more proactive or adaptable, to being more collaborative or quick to learn.

Hard skills: Volunteering is also a great way to pick up practical new skills that can help your career progression. These could include learning IT programs, or gaining experience of a particular task – such as writing press releases or working with specific groups. It can also include gaining accredited training or qualifications as you volunteer. As well as learning new skills, you may also discover ones that you didn't know you had. By getting stuck into a volunteering position, you could find that you have a particular aptitude for a certain way of working, or an untapped skill that you could use in a paid role.

Employability: If you can show a future employer that you've volunteered regularly, it demonstrates your commitment and dependability. Your track record as a volunteer is a powerful way to show many attributes as a candidate, including flexibility, professional behaviour and reliability.

Build a network: Rightly or wrongly, there's a lot of truth in the maxim 'It's not what you know, it's who you know.' If you're looking to develop a rewarding, purposeful career, it can be incredibly valuable to surround yourself with like-minded people who have made that step – and could be a valuable source of advice, contacts and insight. As a volunteer, you may find yourself in a position to network with a wide range of people within an organization. Make sure you build as many relationships as you can – whether someone can help you find work directly, or vouch for your professionalism as a reference to a future employer, you never know when your contacts will come in handy.

If you choose carefully, it's possible to find a single volunteering experience that can give you all of these benefits. For example, if you're a nursing student, there could be many benefits to working for a charity that helps care for elderly people. You can develop your nursing practice on the job, gain (and be able to demonstrate) team-working skills, and prove your flexibility and adaptability to a future employer. From problem solving to communication skills, this kind of volunteer opportunity can enable you to gain and evidence a variety of skills and experiences, and you may come into contact with many peers and senior professionals who can help you on your career journey.

How to choose a volunteering opportunity

There are literally thousands of opportunities to volunteer your time to good causes – so how do you narrow down the options, and find the right positions?

Start with passion
It sounds simple, but it's important that you share the organization's values. Don't choose to volunteer somewhere for the sake of experience alone. If you don't really believe in the project or cause, it can be hard to maintain your enthusiasm or seize the opportunities in front of you, and can sometimes cause friction or resentment.

Be realistic

How much time can you give? It's essential to be realistic upfront about your commitment – and to make sure that you can stick to it. If you're a no-show or the quality of your work suffers because you're stretched too thin, it will make a bad impression.

Think skills

Volunteering may not be paid, but it can be an excellent opportunity to pick up new skills. Whether you're looking to gain experience helping to manage teams, running events, or learning practical new skills – such as a new software program – choose the volunteer opportunities that could help you take on some responsibility and get hands-on experience which could look good on your CV.

Understand your offer

The great thing about a volunteering role is that you don't always need qualifications or experience to put a foot in the door. Think of all the skills you have – not just your formal credentials. What do you have to offer? And what would you most like to be doing day-to-day? If you can find a role that you're likely to be good at, you're also more likely to enjoy it and do well.

Create your own volunteering role

You don't always have to go for an advertised volunteering role. If there is something you know you can do, but you need experience in actually doing it, why not be proactive and ask around? You never know – an organization may actually need your skills even if they don't advertise for them. Pitch the idea to their volunteering team.

Changing a voluntary role into paid work

You know why volunteering makes sense. You've even found a great opportunity to get involved. How do you use it to help you move up the ethical careers ladder? Here are some tips.

Be patient

Some people are very lucky – they're in the right place at the right time when a paid role comes up. But you may need to spend a little time proving yourself. And even if an organization does want to hire you, they may not be able to afford to do so straight away. Stay focused, and make sure they know you are committed.

Three tips for effective volunteering

Debbie Hill is head of volunteering at the charity Marie Curie. Here are her top three pieces of advice for volunteers:

1 **Be true to your motivations** for volunteering – this is where your energy and passion is and this will help you achieve success faster but don't shut the door on an opportunity too fast without considering the opportunity first.

2 **Be proactive** – success won't be handed to you on a plate. Contact people, use the internet and volunteer centres, sell yourself, be clear on what your achievements and abilities are and how you can demonstrate these.

3 **Network** – once you are in a volunteering role, get out and meet people. Give yourself time to reflect on what you are experiencing and the skills you are developing and utilize the staff and other volunteers around you. And always remember the huge and wonderful impact you are making by volunteering, and be proud of that.

Source: The Guardian

Be indispensable

Get stuck in. Take on responsibilities. Be the person that gets things done, reliably and without fuss. The more reliant they become on you, the more reluctant they will be to see you go – and the more likely it is you'll be considered for paid work.

Build relationships

Talk to everyone. You never know when opportunities can arise – and it's just as likely to be over an impromptu coffee as in a meeting. And if you leave a volunteering role, stay in touch with people. You never know when a new role might come up – and you need to be at the forefront of their minds.

Stay humble

You may want to change the world, but remember that you're a volunteer for now. By wanting to show the organization your strengths, there's a temptation to want to make a huge impact straight away. Enthusiasm is great, but no-one wants to work with someone who seems overpowering or too full of their own ego.

Accept that you may be expected to do any number of tasks that fall well beneath your level of expertise. Showing a sense of willingness, adaptability and competence is more important than trying to outsmart or outshine the existing team.

Be professional

Give your volunteering role the same respect you would give a paid role. That means taking pride in your work and showing true commitment. When the time comes to hire new staff, they will remember your professionalism.

Make your intentions clear

Tell your boss up front that you'd eventually like to move to full-time work. If they don't know, then they won't know to consider you for paid positions. They may even want to give you specific duties to train you up for a paid position they have in mind, or fast-track you to employment.

Jessica's story

Idealist is a global non-profit organization that connects people who want to do good in the world to opportunities for action. Although predominantly US-based, it's an excellent resource, and the following story of one volunteer shows that it's possible to turn unpaid opportunities into paid roles.

Living in Nashville, Tennessee, 23-year-old Jessica Thibodeaux was taking a break from college and looking for a way to give back. She never expected that a volunteer gig would lead not only to a paid position, but also a change in perspective about her career path.

'I couldn't afford to go to [university], but I knew that, no matter what, I needed to put my effort into doing something,' she said. 'A lot of people forget about volunteering because it does require a lot of time and effort, and you could make money somewhere else. I just wanted to get the experience and it ended up paying off more than I ever expected.'

While working at another job, Jessica saw a volunteer position at the Crisis Line, part of Family and Children's Service (F&CS), in the summer of 2012, but was unable to attend the training at the time. Instead, she started volunteering for I'm Alive, an online crisis chat network: she received training, took a class and gained a certification for such crisis-line work. When the next round of training came up

More top volunteering tips

Emma Seymour is the head of volunteering strategy and management at the Sussex-based charity hospice Martlets. Here are her top five tips for volunteering effectively:

- **Be clear** about what it is that you want to get out of the volunteering experience. Is it exposure to a certain environment or a new sector? Is it gaining experience in using a new skill? If this is top of your list, be clear about this in offering your time so as to be sure you get what you need.

- Make sure you know what the **role requires** you to do. Ask for a role description and cross-check as you would with a person spec when applying for a job and considering if it is right for you. Volunteering is your choice so you need to be fully informed about the boundaries.

- **Be proactive** in the matching process – if you know that you only have a few hours a week or month, focus your time on roles that specify this. If you need a certain level of supervision or support, be clear about what you need and ask if this is available. Don't leave it up to chance.

- Think about the **springboard effect**. For example, our retail volunteers frequently go on to secure paid positions in our shops as shop assistants or assistant managers. Our professionally skilled volunteers may want to give something back – for example by offering reiki – but, through volunteering with a hospice, they gain specific experience of using this professional skill with a unique cohort of people. That can help them in their careers. We often also have pre-medical students volunteering to serve the teas on the In-Patient Unit simply to gain exposure to a clinical environment without undertaking a clinical role. This really stands in their favour when applying for university – we lose many of them as they are so successful!

- Consider **sending in your CV** and offering *pro bono* services as a volunteer. You may get more from this approach than simply trying to fit yourself into the volunteering opportunities you can find out there. For example, many charities would often hope to use the skills of volunteers far more widely than you'd find in a specific role. Here at Martlets, for example, a receptionist may also offer her time as a project manager if she has those skills.

for the Crisis Line at F&CS, Jessica jumped at the chance, and found that many of her recently learned skills translated.

'The training with F&CS on the crisis line was extremely similar,' she explained. 'We talked about the QPR method [Question, Persuade, Refer], and before they even got to it, I brought it up. The methods and procedures were almost the same thing I'm Alive does. That prepared me, and they could see it.'

Her skills translated so much, in fact, that her supervisor came to her only a month after she started training with F&CS and two weeks after starting the actual volunteering, to tell her about an open paid position and to encourage her to apply.

'The organization is really great at identifying people, and their qualities, work ethic and knowledge. They notice good workers and people who know their stuff and who can do a good job,' Jessica said.

The organization used to provide just adoption services, but has expanded into counselling and community services in recent years, she added. Jessica has watched social workers throughout the organization use their degrees and experience, and has been inspired.

'It has definitely changed my opinion about the direction I want to go with university,' Jessica said. 'When I started volunteering, I saw the hands-on work that the social workers do. Watching the people who do have a social-work background at my job, I get to see exactly how they use their degree and what they do with it.'

Source: idealistcareers.org

If you're thinking about volunteering to help you move up the ethical career ladder, I hope this chapter has given you some food for thought on how to use your time effectively.

In the next, final chapter, we'll show where this can lead – by meeting some more people who have been guided by their ethical principles and found work they love.

They did it

and so can you!

They did it – and so can you!

You've now read about some of the many approaches to finding – and succeeding in – a career that makes a positive impact on the world.

I hope you're feeling informed and inspired to take your next step and find work you love.

If you need any more encouragement that a purposeful career is achievable – and worth the effort – this chapter is here to help.

From farmers to marketers, charity workers to managing directors, let's meet a few more people who have 'been there and done it' – and see what advice they have to share.

Alyson Walsh

Director of Marketing & Campaigns, FareShare

'I wanted a role with a purpose, but it had to be linked to the thing that makes me tick.'

What do you do?
I work for FareShare – an environmental organization that ensures surplus food gets to frontline charities around the UK. We aim to support the organizations that put people on the path to rehabilitation.

Is it enjoyable?
It's fantastic. We've just started working with the Women's Institute, and are contributing to the conversation around food waste and food poverty. I'm also shaping a new marketing and volunteering strategy for the organization. There are 101 things going on!

How did you get here?
I was marketing manager at [luxury food store] Fortnum and Mason's – which was just a bit different! But food was the common denominator. I wanted a role with a purpose, but it had to be linked to the thing that makes me tick.

Were you always motivated by principles?
Yes, I campaigned for Amnesty

International at university, and always felt that there was too much injustice in the world. I wanted to make things better. After uni, I approached some cancer charities and they told me to go away and get some commercial experience. That's what I did. I spent three years at [cosmetics company] Wella in their marketing and product division.

What's the best advice you've had?

Well, it's a bit unusual, but my go-to person for philosophy is Ivana Trump. She says, 'It is what is' – if something doesn't work, then move on. I like that. My father used to say 'Principles don't put food on the table.' I think that's partly a generational thing – and I don't believe it. Our core principle is putting food on the table! I know he'd be happy to be wrong.

What advice would you give?

If you want to pursue a career in marketing with a purpose, it's helpful to have a varied background. Get the skills first. Marketing is a broad church but you can become very specialist working in communications organizations. Organizations with purpose tend to need more generalists – as they may not have huge teams. So be as multi-skilled as you can, and connect with what it is that makes you tick.

FareShare: **fareshare.org.uk**

Dominique De-Light

Founder & Director, Creative Future

'My job has gone from being a creative-writing teacher to building an entire organization.'

Where did your ethical career journey start?

Probably when I went to Trinidad and began writing. It was such a culture shock moving from the north of England to the Caribbean. I began writing for myself initially, but ended up getting the job to write the *Rough Guide to Trinidad & Tobago*. It was chutzpah really – I got in touch, and they asked for some writing samples. My co-writer had to apply with 1,000 other people.

What was your spark?

Writing about Trinidad, I came across a lot of social injustice. I'd always been an artist in some way, and now I wanted to make a difference. When I came back to England, I did a creative writing MA. But I had to earn a living and didn't have any contacts in journalism, so I started teaching adult education. I found that quite tedious.

Did you volunteer?

Yes. I first began volunteer teaching at the *Brighton Big Issue* – I think the people there taught me as much as I taught them. And I found it so rewarding. So I went to a local homeless day centre, suggested starting a writing group and applied for funding from the Arts Council.

How did you start Creative Future?

I showed the Arts Council that there were lots of talented but intimidated people with no access to the mainstream arts – and, in the end, I got three years' funding to manage 11 artists.

Someone told me I should be running an organization, not just a day centre. I said I was a writer, not a project manager – but then I met someone with a similar background who'd moved to Brighton, and we just went with our instincts and started the charity.

Where are you now?

In 10 years, we've worked with around 4,000 marginalized artists and writers. My job has gone from being a creative writing teacher to building an entire organization.

It is a worthwhile job. It's fantastic talking to artists who say they've changed their lives – people who were heroin addicts and homeless, and now have won writing awards, and gone on to do degrees.

How have you made a difference?

I wanted to change the world through my writing and art, but I'm actually making an impact in a different way. I am very proud of that, but I still want to write. I've always insisted that I wouldn't work more than three days a week, so I would have time for my creative work. It's really important for my integrity – and keeps me in touch with the challenges of trying to be a creative practitioner.

Would you recommend it?

This job is extremely challenging. It can be stressful managing other people, and – as a charity – you're constantly having to find funds. I don't think I could be in the voluntary sector unless I believed in what the organization stood for.

I think I would struggle with working for anyone in the private sector. I'd be asking myself, why am I working so hard to put more money in someone else's pocket? That's not what I'm interested in. What motivates me is changing people's lives.

Creative Future: **creativefuture.org.uk**

Rachel Egan

Marketing Executive, Charities Aid Foundation (CAF)

'I can't imagine moving out of the charity sector. You can make a real social impact and meet a lot of like-minded people.'

How did you get started?

I went to Cardiff University and began volunteering there. I got involved in the mental-health society and set up an eating-disorder service. I was mostly doing marketing and communications, as well as some campaigning.

I became a trustee of a charity at 20, which is pretty young. I had personal experience of those mental-health issues, and that was a huge motivator. It really helped build self-esteem and it was amazing to win awards for services to the Students' Union.

What happened next?

I did a 10-month placement at university – helping 80 students to get internships at charities. We'd pitch the scheme to charities, who would help train the interns in different areas. I was still volunteering but then began working at a market research agency for the charity sector. I also trained as a mentor for the organization Mindful, and started helping children with mental-health problems. So I was doing voluntary work and mentoring, but now getting paid for it as well – it was all starting to blur into one!

What do you do now?

I am now a marketing executive for the Charities Aid Foundation. I support the private client team – which means working with wealthy philanthropists who open and use trusts to give money to good causes. I'm still volunteering as a mentor in my spare time, and have been supporting people with anorexia, anxiety and depression for many years.

What are the pros and cons of working for a charity?

I can't imagine moving out of the charity sector. You can make a real social impact and meet a lot of like-minded people. I also feel it can be easier to progress – I went from a volunteer to a trustee in nine months. I would definitely recommend becoming a trustee as you get to understand how all parts of a charity come together – from legal and financial to operational. Not a lot of young people understand how charities work!

The downside is that pay does tend to be a lot lower [than the private sector], and a lot of charity jobs are on short-term contracts. I'm now in a permanent role, but I had three years of contracting and it was hard to have that insecurity.

How to get started

If you're thinking about taking a step into the charity world, make sure you really care – and that it's not just for your CV. Because I was so passionate about a cause, that was all the reward I needed.

I also think it's okay to start small. If you're volunteering or working for a large charity, it can be hard to see your impact. At a tiny charity, you can see it instantly, and it can be massive.

Charities Aid Foundation: cafonline.org

Siobhan Riordan

Energy and Sustainability Manager, ISS

'Good communication is a key skill... if you can't communicate well and get people to believe in you, it undoes a lot of your hard work.'

Tell us about what you do

ISS are a facilities management company and they employ me specifically to work for one of their biggest clients in the financial sector. I manage energy and sustainability in their premises across Europe.

Where did you start out?

I majored in Environmental Science and I really struggled to find a job after uni. I knew I wanted to be environmentally friendly, but I was so blinkered about being a conservationist and trying to save the world. I soon realized I was competing with people who had PhDs, for a £12,000-a-year job working at the Environment Agency digging up mud samples. I spent six months doing volunteer work in the conservation sector, but I was so broke that I had to find a properly paid job.

Most potential employers saw my degree title and said, 'If you had a [mainstream] science degree we'd consider you but you're just not ticking the boxes.' Eventually, a consultancy took me on assessing workplaces for water quality, air quality and health & safety.

How did you move from health & safety to sustainability?

My employers eventually let me focus more on environmental services – for example, the 14001 environmental management standard. They said, 'If you can sell it, you can do it.' So then I had to go out and sell it to clients.

The demand for environmental services grew, and that led my employer to pay for me to train as a low-carbon energy assessor through a government scheme. I think this accreditation has opened a lot of doors for me. I became a sustainability advisor for my next employer and spent four years writing their corporate responsibility report.

What difference do you think you're making?

I only really wanted work where I would make a difference – if I stop making a difference at work I feel really frustrated and move on to something else. Now that I'm working in energy consumption I feel I'm making a difference just by bringing my previous experience as a consultant.

I've saved my client money, made them more energy efficient, they're producing less waste and using less water. By the end of the year I can say, 'We've saved this amount of money and this many tonnes of carbon.' That's what I do it for, really. I can see we've made an impact.

It's great when you make a change and then you see that same change happen throughout a country or throughout Europe. It's almost like starting a trend. We could do something really innovative in a European office, and then they might follow it on for their offices in other parts of the world, and then other businesses in those countries might take it on too.

What is it like to be ethical in a corporate environment?

My client looks at what I do as an output. So I can spend a lot of time doing all kinds of things, but I'll often just be judged on a graph that says we've made a reduction. They want quantifiable figures, rather than the more fluffy side of energy saving. And it's really difficult to get any business to think about what it's going to be like in 20 years, so it's a bit of a fight to get them to spend money on sustainability projects!

My boss at my last job jokingly called me a 'tree-hugger' which I actually found pretty funny. But I've often had to get over that mindset and say, 'It's not just about tree-hugging, I'm actually trying to save you money and make the business more efficient.'

What is your top tip for career seekers?

I think good communication is a key skill. You could be great at setting up procedures and thinking up ideas, but if you can't communicate well and get people to believe in you, it undoes a lot of your hard work. Energy and sustainability is one of those areas where people are doing it because they think they should – and, if they don't understand something, they'll think you're trying to fluff around it and won't take you seriously.

Sustainability at ISS:
issworld.com/corporate-responsibility

Valeria Vargas

Education for Sustainable Development Co-ordinator, Manchester Metropolitan University

'It wasn't like a plan – it was more like it was something I was passionate about.'

Tell us about what you do

My role is about finding ways to help the process of embedding education for sustainable development within the university curriculum.

Why does it make you happy?

I see it as something meaningful and something that can really make a difference. I feel that I have finally found what I want to do in my life and the change I want to make. And because I've found that, it doesn't really feel like a job.

When did that passion start?

Ever since I was little I was very interested in the environment. My mother worked in research in the Amazon rainforest and we lived there for a little while. I learned a lot about indigenous thinking and practices there, and how to live in the forest, so that was where I learned about the environmental side of sustainability.

Have you always worked in environmental sustainability?

No, my degree was in music, and then I worked freelance for several years in the music and arts sector. I was more on the social side of sustainability – and it's been very varied. I volunteered at a hospital in Colombia, I've worked with women affected by violence, and as a consultant with NGOs, and I've worked with many up-and-coming artists at an art gallery.

While I was working at the gallery I completed an MA in Contemporary Curating, but then I left to have a child. I think I wasn't meant to be a curator or a musician – I wasn't very good at either! Both my degrees were really hard work.

And then, when I wanted to go back to work, I struggled to find a job. Things are quite different in the UK compared with Colombia – the work culture and the way you do applications.

How did you make the jump from the arts to environmental sustainability education?

I did a paid internship through Manchester Metropolitan University (MMU) at the art school – I thought it would help me learn about the working culture here and then afterwards I would be able to get another job. It was really good because they let me create the whole project that I was working on.

It was similar to what I do now – finding ways to engage staff and students in environmental sustainability.

While I was there, MMU created what is now my current job and I applied for it. For a while it was just contract-based and then finally they made it permanent after I'd shown that my role could be beneficial long-term.

What difference do you think you're making?

I know people are quite cy nical about it, but I do think that things are changing and improving. And there is a need for more people working towards that – and not just working for the sake of earning money.

Is embedding sustainability into education a good way to create a global impact?

Yes. But it wasn't like a plan – it was more like it was something I was passionate about. I didn't really go to the job interview thinking I was going to change the world!

Looking back, is there anything you would have done differently?

I wish I could have worried less about how things are going to pan out.

And maybe it would be better to have a degree in the thing you're actually doing, but I also think it's good to have a multi-disciplinary career.

What top tips do you have for someone seeking a career that's about more than money?

Be very open-minded, because you can find some really nice surprises. For example, I never thought that the internship was going to lead me to this job.

I used to go for roles that were similar to what I was doing previously – but maybe that wasn't the best fit. I feel comfortable in my current role, even if it doesn't align to the other parts of my career.

Manchester Metropolitan University: **mmu.ac.uk**

Paula Luu

Former senior manager at Net Impact (and current MBA student at the University of Michigan)

'We can't all be CSR directors but there is a way for you to fold your personal values into the work you do.'

What does an ethical career mean to you?

It's about authenticity – living out a career that upholds personal values of people, community, environment and business.

When did you decide you wanted an ethical career?

The turning point for me came when I was working as a contractor for a PR agency in San Francisco after I'd graduated.

My whole education (in Psychology and Consumer Science) was building up to this kind of job. It was challenging work with intelligent people but I felt so unfulfilled I'd go home and cry.

At the peak of the recession in 2010 I turned down a full-time job and instead went to work for free as an intern at Rainforest Action Network (RAN). At 22 I was organizing nonviolent protests against big oil companies to reduce air pollution and consumer education drives against the production of palm oil.

Tell us about Net Impact

It's an amazing community of more than 100,000 students and young professionals who want to transform their passions into world-changing action.

I joined the organization because of its culture and community. It's been around for 23 years but feels like a start up. I was quite upfront about my skillset around PR and media, but that it wasn't where I wanted to see myself. It worked out perfectly – I moved from marketing into organizational growth and strategy, and ended up leading Net Impact's work to establish new chapters around the world, and recruit new students. And when I decided to take my next step, they were very supportive.

What are you doing now?

My ideology has changed significantly since my days at Rainforest Action Network. The scale that business has to enact change is huge, positive or not. And to be an impact leader in order to support people, planet and communities, you have to flex those business muscles. I deliberately decided not to pursue an MBA specifically in Sustainability because I need to learn the language and thinking of traditional business if I'm going to change it. I also wanted to challenge myself.

Is there anything you would have done differently?

I didn't network or surround myself with a community of like-minded people (outside of Monday to Friday co-workers) during my first two years of working. There's something powerful about doing that. I'd have plugged myself into a network of people who could challenge and encourage me to explore different avenues. If I had done that I would have got to where I am now sooner.

Also, working on sustainability can be taxing. I read so much awful news and think, 'What's the point?' That's inevitable, so it's important to surround yourself with people who share similar views.

What tips do you have for someone seeking an ethical career?

We can't all be CSR directors or sustainability project managers, but there is a way to fold in your personal values into the work you do, whether you're an accountant, a software engineer or a janitor.

The hardest but most important part is sitting down and asking yourself what really matters and figuring out the answers. Then it's all about living every day authentically, including your career.

Net Impact: **netimpact.org**

Nikki Gatenby

Managing Director of search marketing agency Propellernet

'I believe that, if you put people and purpose first, profit will come.'

How did you get started?

I climbed the career ladder fast. I was an account director at a London advertising agency at the age of 25, a client-services director with a team of a hundred shortly after. I helped win the company a huge contract worth millions of pounds.

Although it was fun, it was also intense – I was on 90-hour weeks, I'd not had a weekend off for a long time. My fitness levels were through the floor and my social life was in serious need of resuscitation. And one morning I woke up literally unable to move.

Luckily, it wasn't a heart attack – but it was my body's way of telling me to calm down and do something different.

What did you do?

I resigned. I spent some time travelling around South America. And, when I came back, I started a new chapter with Propellernet.

We've made it our personal mission

to succeed as a business without anyone becoming a crash or a burnout statistic. Our whole ethos, our whole reason for being, is enjoying the workplace. We fundamentally believe that if you help people achieve their dreams, you will definitely win their hearts and minds.

How did you find your guiding principle?

I saw the Olympic rower Ben Hunt-Davis give a talk about his crew's philosophy, which was: 'Will it make the boat go faster?' It was such a simple line, but it was central to everything they did. From what they ate to how they trained, everything was to make the boat go faster.

At Propellernet, our mantra is 'Make life better'. And we do the same thing. We're always asking: how will this make a difference?

It's a real mind shift. A lot of advertising and marketing agencies are just in pursuit of cold hard cash. But I believe that, if you put people and purpose first, profit will come.

In *The Happy Manifesto* – a great book about engagement at work – author Henry Stewart cites a global survey stating that only one person in 20 is actually engaged in their job. I like to think we've flipped this around with Propellernet – and I'm very proud that we've been recognized as one of the best places to work in the UK for the last four years running.

What do you look for in an employee?

When I interview someone, I ask them to show me what's innovative, I want to know what they enjoy about innovation. I want them to show me their sense of creativity, and know what their spirit of adventure is like. Are they fun to work with? Do they look after themselves (that's really important)? If we can engage, from a values perspective, that's the first step in having a great place to work.

What are your three top pieces of advice?

Listen to your heart and all the dreams within it because, I know from experience, it might stop. Second, rest before you're tired – I really wish someone had said this to me when I was younger; because if you don't rest you could crash and burn. We're human, we're not androids – we're meant to take time out. Finally, dance to the beat of your own drum – and find people who share that beat.

Propellernet: **propellernet.co.uk**

Topher Campbell

Theatre director, filmmaker and writer

'I wanted to make choices that made me happy. And I wanted to make a difference in the world.'

What were your early ambitions?
I had a difficult background – I was abandoned at one-and-a-half and grew up in children's homes and foster care. As I grew older, I had no sense of my racial or sexual identity. And one day my schoolteacher took me to a university open day – and I thought, 'Well, if they think I should be here, perhaps I should be'. From that moment, I realized there was another possibility.

How did life change?
I went to university and joined the drama society. When I left, I saw an advert for a young theatre directors' training scheme in *The Guardian*. I didn't realize you could do that professionally – I thought it was just something you did for fun.

Did you have set ambitions?
When I was around 21, I began thinking what I wanted to do with my life. I knew it wasn't going to be just about making money – doing things in a textbook way. I never imagined I'd work in an office. But I did know I wanted to make choices that made me happy. And I wanted to make a difference in the world.

What were your motivations?
I felt that the world wasn't the way it should be for people like me – someone who was black and had a different sexuality. I wanted to do something that mattered. I came up against a lot of barriers but I pushed through them.

How did you start out?
I began training as a director, and got an assistant director job at the National Theatre – but it wasn't full time. So I also did modelling, was a cycle courier, waited tables – anything that didn't involve commitment. I didn't want to think that I had to go and work at a company because I didn't have money.

Where did rukus! come from?
I made my first film at 27 about my best friend. We wanted to create something where black people didn't feel like victims. We were all about self-determination. And that's where the idea of rukus! came from – an arts company dedicated to presenting work by Black Lesbian, Gay, and Bisexual, Transgender (BLGBT) artists. Together we built the UK's first and only BLGBT Archive, which is now housed at the London Metropolitan Archive.

Have things always gone to plan?
No. There were times when I was

unemployed – and I sometimes preferred that. If you're offered a job and it's just about the money, you're going to be unhappy. The flipside of being an outsider is that you're free and can make choices. That's what happened when I took on the Red Room Theatre Company. There was virtually no money, but it was just what I wanted to do – and we spent seven years creating experimental film, theatre and writing.

Where did you focus your attention?

One area was climate change. With the Oikos Project I was thinking – if you had children – how could you tell them what it was like when environmental disasters happen? We couldn't leave it to leaders and government, when they'd been so ineffectual about it. We built the UK's first fully functioning recycled theatre. It was a huge collaboration, and very politically motivated.

What attributes have you needed?

You need to have bravery and patience. You may know that you have the skill and vision, but those two things will always be challenged. If you're brave, you'll continue to do what you want – and if you're patient, you can live through the tough times, and people pressuring you to do things you don't want. If you have a sense that your true north doesn't have to be the same as everyone else's, then you're onto a winner.

Did you imagine you'd succeed in this career?

I think you have instincts when you're young. And if you persevere with them, you'll find the toolbox you need to keep moving forward. On an individual level, you always need to keep having conversations with yourself. There may be personal issues – family, relationships, money – that don't support it. And sometimes you have to do things you don't want to. But you keep sharpening your toolbox.

Where do you find inspiration?

There are so many people I admire, living and dead. And because of them, you can never really make an excuse that you can't do things. The world is full of amazing people who have added to the world in ways that you or I could only dream of. So we can each just carry on!

What advice would you share?

One of my mantras is live, love and leave a legacy. For me, if you say to yourself, 'I need to go out and earn £100,000 because that will make me happy', no-one can say if that's right or wrong. But if you say, 'I want to have an interesting life, and do interesting things' then you'll be constantly surprised by the things you come across, the people you meet and the places you go. That's what makes it worthwhile.

Rukus: **rukus.org.uk**

Fiona Cromwell

*Marketing and Fundraising Officer,
Designability*

'The cause is also very important. It has to be something I feel strongly about.'

How did you get your first job?

I did quite a general degree – it was in Cultural and Media Studies – so there wasn't really a clear career pathway. After graduating, I applied for a role with a local charity in Wiltshire. I began working in information development – mostly helping unpaid carers to learn about the respite care that they could get.

What happened next?

The charity amalgamated with another organization – and that gave me an opportunity to take on a new position. I stepped up into a communications role, which was great. As a new charity, they had to develop their profile and focus more on communications. I really enjoyed that experience and it helped with my next step. Last year, I applied for a role as marketing officer at another charity, Designability. We research and design products that help people living with disabilities.

So you've only worked for charities?

Yes. In some ways, I've just simply wanted to stay in the sector – as it feels right for me. But the cause is also very important. It has to be something that I feel strongly about.

Are you earning less than you could in the private sector?

Probably yes! I think I'm blessed and cursed. I do feel that I'm doing something very meaningful, but I know there's not big money in this.

Does that frustrate you?

Yes and no. I am always looking to further myself – so I'm ambitious in one sense. But it isn't just about the career for me – there's more to life than that. I want everything to align: my work, the area I choose to live in and my personal life.

What's your advice to people looking for work at a charity?

I would say volunteering is very important, and it's good if you can show that commitment. But I believe a huge part of it is personality fit – are you the right person for the organization? If you're interested in a charity, try to find out how they work and what the dynamics are. You could have a lot of experience, but if the character fit isn't right, that will eliminate you from the selection process very quickly.

Designabilty: **designability.org.uk**

Amy Nicholls

Sustainability Strategy Officer,
Network Rail

'My advice would be to simply ask someone for a coffee – you never know where it can lead.'

What do you do now?

I help manage the social performance of Network Rail – the authority responsible for the UK railway network. Before I started, they were very good and clear about their environmental impact, but they didn't have a joined-up approach to measuring the organization's social impact. This is a very new and exciting area.

How did you get here?

My career path was really a succession of accidents until my mid-thirties. The common thread was working in communications. But I went from working at a retail business to doing PR for the London Film Festival. They were short stints, and usually came through my network of friends and contacts.

When did you first find a more lasting role?

In my mid-twenties, I heard about an opportunity at PriceWaterhouseCoopers (PwC) through a friend, and that was the start of a successful nine-year career there. I became more involved in business development, spent a lot

of time abroad – and moved up the ladder. I ended up managing a team of 40 people.

Why did you change?

I had a clear career progression ahead of me, and knew I would be rewarded financially. But I hit a point when I felt it wasn't right. I was working incredibly hard, but it was all essentially to win work for partners in that organization. I had a brilliant time at PwC and learned a lot, but I thought that can't be the purpose of my life!

How did you time the jump?

I made a clean break in 2013. It was a pretty renegade decision but I knew I had to do it. And, a little randomly, I decided to volunteer back at the London Film Festival. I'd worked there in 2003, and I liked the idea of going back 10 years later.

By chance, I met someone whose husband was working in sustainability. We met for a coffee, we realized I had transferable skills in business development, and I started doing consultancy work for his business. And one day he called to say a client needed help and would I meet them? That was Network Rail.

Did you start full-time?

No – I was very flexible and began contracting three days a week, working to a daily rate. But I soon moved into a full-time position.

What do you most enjoy about the role?

Working in professional services at PwC couldn't be more different from the railways – and some people think it's an odd career move. But it's actually amazing.

With a consultancy project like PwC, the work can be so cerebral and abstract – it's almost unreal. And the railways are totally opposite: it's incredibly tangible, and you are incredibly aware of helping people to get around Britain.

Are you a natural fit?

Ha, not really – I'm surrounded by railway experts and engineers. But I actually quite like being part of an 'alternative thinking' team in an otherwise relatively bland environment. I think it may even help me to be more creative.

What advice would you give to someone looking for an ethical career?

My whole life has been about networks. My friends joke that I'm a human LinkedIn. But it's true – I do try to find connections for people, and it's really important to be connected. Especially in the ethical careers world, you can find that some communities are still quite small, that people may feel a little alone in their roles, and that they're more than happy to talk about their experiences.

If you're interested in a particular role, my advice would be to simply ask someone working in that area for a coffee – you never know where it can lead. You'd be surprised how open many people will be in talking about what they're doing, and what can come from something as simple as meeting for a coffee.

Network Rail: **networkrail.co.uk**

Ravinol Chambers,

Social purpose video producer,
Be Inspired Films

'I committed early on that I wanted the business to stand on its own two feet – without any funding or grants.'

Did you always want to do good?

No. As a teenager in Dublin, I wanted to be a stockbroker! My main aim was to be a millionaire and have a fancy car.

What changed?

In my school we had a personal development year [when we were 16]. We went on retreats, did creative writing and had group discussions about big issues. It was a real time of exploration – and I realized I wanted to do something meaningful with my life.

What did you specialize in?

I studied Psychology at university because I wanted to understand more what life was all about. I really wanted to study happiness. After that, I became a full-time Hare Krishna monk. I travelled across the world, helping to put on cultural festivals. It was immensely fulfilling – a real life of dedication.

Why did you stop?

At 29, I realized it would be hard to maintain that life. If I wanted to get married, I needed a job. So I basically started again then – about 10 years behind most people.

Did you keep to your values?

Not immediately. The business side of me kicked back in. I worked as an estate agent for a few years, and did well. I needed that financial security – but then I was drawn back in to helping communities.

How did you start in film?

I'd made one film before [as a monk] in East Africa about a school for street kids. I shot it on a Hi8 video camera and edited it on two VHS machines. And when I took on a new job – as a project manager running mentoring projects with kids at risk of exclusion – I made another video. That sparked something.

Did you start a business then?

No. I first decided to go to university and do an MBA. But it was business as unusual because I specialized in venture philanthropy. There had always been an idea that business somehow justified people doing horrible things. If you wanted to make money, then it was okay to be an asshole.

But venture philanthropy turned that on its head. Businesspeople were using their skills and intelligence to see how they could make charitable giving more effective. The MBA introduced me to lots of leading people in the field; it also gave me kudos, and enabled me to talk to people at the right level.

Tell us about starting Be Inspired Films?

I was tempted to follow the classic MBA route – and earn lots of money. But what pulled me back was the need to do something with impact. [Apple co-founder] Steve Jobs said that innovation lies in the intersection between seemingly unconnected things. For him it was art and technology. For me, it's film and video with social impact. I wasn't the first to think of it, but it wasn't a big sector at the time.

How were the early days?

Tough. I earned £10,000 for the first two years, but I stuck to my values. We made ourselves very visible, insisted on creating excellent work and made some strategic partnerships. I committed early on that I wanted the business to stand on its own two feet – without any funding or grants. The work should be good enough to pay me for it.

And it paid off.

What do you now?

Be Inspired is a multi-award-winning video production company that helps individuals and organizations who are working as a force for good across business and society to bring their stories to life. This is an exciting time for us.

What's your advice for ethical job seekers?

I was always told it's good to be niche. The fear is always that you'll exclude people – but for those people you want to work with, you're a million times more attractive. You may get less of the pie, but you get a deeper piece.

That can be true but I do also think that charities and social enterprises can only ever make a dent in the corner of the universe. If you want to make a real impact, it's all about affecting the mainstream. The idea of 'us and them' – of business being bad – is old thinking and very short sighted. It doesn't help the dialogue and, even if it were true, the only way to change it is to work from the inside. That's a good place to be.

Be Inspired Films: **beinspireduk.org**

Roly and Camilla Puzey

Tenant farmers, Saddlescombe Farm

'We do it because we love what we do.'

How did your passion for farming start?

We both grew up in farming families, but didn't have any access to land. So we both did lots of other jobs before realizing our hearts really were in the country.

Today, we run Saddlescombe Farm as a traditional sheep, beef and arable farm. We produce the best-quality meat through high animal welfare, protecting and enhancing the natural environment. And we involve the local community through farm visits and open days.

What were you doing before?

(Camilla) I did a degree in History and Spanish, and then went to work in an auction house in London, before teaching English as a foreign language in Spain and London. But having the privilege of growing up in the countryside has a big impact on your outlook and on where you want to live.

After a few years I did a farming course, and then began working for two different farming charities: the Farming & Wildlife Advisory Group (FWAG) and LEAF (Linking Environment And Farming). That's where I met Roly.

Did that draw you back to the country?

Yes, we were running workshops to help farmers host farm visits and increase public awareness at the time. I was also writing guidelines on environmentally friendly farming, and eventually we realized that we wanted to give farming a go ourselves.

How did you start?

We got onto a scheme called Farm Step, run by the charity Earth Trust. It's designed to help people without a tenancy to get onto the farming ladder, and it gave us the opportunity to work a bit of land.

From there, we applied to the National Trust for the tenancy of Saddlescombe Farm in Sussex. They wanted someone to live here and bring it back to life. They were keen to have people who were happy to give farm visits and open days, and that's what we've done.

Has it lived up to your expectations?

It's definitely a life project, but we love it. Farming is about food production – but it's also about taking care of the countryside. People often don't realize the work and care that goes into it. We get a huge amount of satisfaction from relaying hedges and seeing the birds nesting in them. This is an incredible place. In summer you can see orchids and other wildflowers. There are skylarks and yellowhammers. If you're lucky you might see a corn bunting. It's also an incredible place for our children to grow up.

Have you had to make many sacrifices?

People often ask us if we can go on holidays. We can, but that's not why we work seven days a week. And you certainly don't go into farming to get rich, but that doesn't drive us. I think we live comfortably, but I'm sure it's not everyone's cup of tea. We do it because we love what we do.

And you're doing it the way you want to?

Yes. We're fortunate to run a traditional farm in a beautiful place. What we have here is a holistic system. It's the right way to ensure we have healthy animals and wildlife on the farm. And we love running the farm visits – especially seeing children walk around during lambing time.

Saddlescombe Farm: camillaandroly.co.uk/saddlescombe-farm

Tokunbo Ajasa-Oluwa

Head of Innovation at Bauer Academy

'It is really crucial to understand who you are.'

How did you get started?

I studied journalism at university and then worked my way up at magazines, from intern to staff writer. But I always had a parallel interest in youth development too, and I wanted to combine that passion with my career aspirations. Given that work is something I'm doing at least 40 hours a week, I've always felt it has to be something I'm passionate about.

What happened next?

I found a charity called Children's Express, which went on to be called Headliners. The idea was to empower young people in media skills so they could tell their own stories. At the time, 75 per cent of coverage of young people in the press was negative. That job was a real sweet spot for me – going out to hard-to-reach environments across London boroughs and setting up journalism projects.

How did that change you?

Well, I saw these kids had the talent

– they just didn't have the right environment or connections. And they didn't have self-belief. Around that time, I came across Jamie Oliver's social enterprise, Fifteen, and that idea just blew my mind. I didn't have a business background but that's when the penny dropped for Catch 22.

What was Catch 22?

It was a leap into the unknown! I set up Catch 22 as a social enterprise to give UK creative industries access to quality young talent from diverse backgrounds. We found aspiring young people with potential, nurtured them and then introduced them to some of the leading businesses in the sector, including Trinity Mirror, *The Economist* and Associated Newspapers.

Did you enjoy it?

It was amazing. By putting myself in that situation, I learned to take risks – and unearthed some qualities I didn't realize I had. I also started to get audacious, and contacted people at the top of the media industry. Tony Elliot, the founder of *Time Out*, was my first mentor. We were only supposed to have a 15-minute chat, but he ended up supporting me for almost two years as I was getting Catch 22 off the ground.

Why did it stop?

Over time, I'd become a workaholic, and I'd never factored profit into the business, as it was never about the money. So I wound it up. That was tough – it felt like giving up a child – but we sold our networks on to like-minded organizations, so it wasn't lost. I'm proud of the impact we had over seven years.

What was your next career move?

Bauer Media was one of Catch 22's clients, and they asked me to head up a new initiative in 2012. At the time, there were record youth unemployment figures, and I helped launch GoThinkBig, an award-winning social action digital platform to enable young people to achieve their career dreams. Over three years, we supported £17 million of paid work through the website and offered over 30,000 career opportunities to young people in the UK.

What do you do now?

When that project moved on, I stayed with Bauer Media – and I'm now working as an intrapreneur within the business. As head of innovation at the Bauer Academy, I've been involved in lots of interesting outreach initiatives – from engaging the memories of pensioners with dementia via photography, to helping young people learn how to do bulletins at radio stations.

What advice would you share?

I think it is really crucial to understand who you are. We're bombarded with seduction messages every day, saying you need to be like this or that. I never had an overarching strategy but I've always made decisions that felt right. And when I started out I took the time to learn about myself. So when it came to my career aspirations, I knew it was important to find something that would improve me, not just a role with an impressive title. I think you need to understand yourself first – to know what naturally appeals to you – and shape your journey around that.

Cecilia Crossley

Founder, From Babies With Love

'Give yourself time to learn – and don't feel the need to rush.'

When did you start on your ethical career path?

It was never a deliberate strategy. I've always had an international perspective. My mum's from Brazil and I went there when I was little. I saw children in the streets, understood inequality and the destruction of the Amazon. It's part of who I am.

So you've always worked in charities?

No, my very first work experience was at the London Stock Exchange, back when it was full of people shouting and swearing! It was fascinating.

I then did a degree in economics, focusing on development – and my first job was with [global accountancy firm] KPMG in the City. At the time, my dad told me, 'Cecilia, infiltrate from within.' Looking back, I think it was his way of telling me to be a social intrapreneur.

How did you escape the City?

I got involved with KPMG's corporate social responsibility (CSR) department, doing *pro bono* work for some great organizations. And then I had an epiphany moment. I realized that the CSR work was the one thing I really loved, but it was the only thing that wasn't in my job description!

My big jump was to VSO (Voluntary Services Overseas). I worked as an internal auditor – and moved my skills to a different market. In the interview, I was able to use a lot of the *pro bono* work to demonstrate my motivation in international development.

Was it an easy move?

Well, I took a hefty pay cut, and it was also a big drop in terms of future income. Being in a long-term relationship definitely helped, as I had that security. People at KMPG were shocked that I would leave, but I had an amazing time at VSO. I travelled the world and learned about global issues at the coalface, not just through newspaper articles. It was a privilege.

What happened next?

I did some qualifications in charity finance, and then a Masters in International Development at the Cass Business School. It was a bit like an MBA for charities. I met so many interesting people with incredible experiences. I learned so much from them.

When did you start your own social enterprise?

Six years ago, I'd just become a parent – and I saw Save the Children's Christmas advert. It completely struck me. A few months later, I was in a baby clothes shop in North London and I thought: 'Why can't I buy these lovely things and help vulnerable children at the same time?'

Charities don't sell new, premium products to the public – and I understand the reasons why. But that doesn't mean that it's not a good idea. So I started writing a business plan for From Babies With Love. As a social enterprise, 100 per cent of our profits fund the care of orphaned and abandoned children around the world.

I dropped to four days a week at VSO (like the risk-averse accountant I was!) so I could work on the business one day a week. And a year after starting it, I finally quit my job and took the plunge!

Did your corporate background help?

Yes. I really value my experience in the City. I feel very comfortable now pitching to corporates, I know what will tick their boxes and I think it's always good to be able to put yourself in other people's shoes.

How has From Babies With Love developed?

We started out with £5,000 in capital, which was my savings, to buy stock. But I soon realized we needed to develop our own label – we needed to be a brand, not just a retailer. By making our own stuff, we've opened up a lot of opportunities, and are making a much bigger difference.

What's your advice for future social entrepreneurs?

Take incremental steps. Give yourself time to learn – and don't feel the need to rush. That has stood us on good ground. We've made a profit from day one – and I've always been adamant about that. All of our profits go to orphaned children, and I'm very mindful of that responsibility. Running a social enterprise can feel overwhelming, but if you break it down into individual steps it feels more manageable.

From Babies With Love:
frombabieswithlove.org

Index

Bold text indicates a case study